Dr. Bob
and
His Library

Other Titles by Dick B.

Anne Smith's Journal, 1933-1939:
A.A.'s Principles of Success

The Oxford Group & Alcoholics Anonymous:
A Design for Living That Works

The Akron Genesis of Alcoholics Anonymous

The Books Early AAs Read for Spiritual Growth

New Light on Alcoholism:
The A.A. Legacy from Sam Shoemaker

Courage to Change (with Bill Pittman)

The Good Book and The Big Book:
A.A.'s Roots in the Bible

That Amazing Grace:
The Role of Clarence and Grace S. in Alcoholics Anonymous

Good Morning!:
Quiet Time, Morning Watch, Meditation, and Early A.A.

Turning Point:
A History of Early A.A.'s Spiritual Roots and Successes

Hope!:
The Story of Geraldine D., Alina Lodge & Recovery

Utilizing Early A.A.'s Spiritual Roots for Recovery Today

Dr. Bob
and
His Library

A Major A.A. Spiritual Source

Dick B.

Foreword to First Edition by Ernest Kurtz, Ph.D.

Paradise Research Publications, Inc.
Kihei, Maui, Hawaii

Paradise Research Publications, Inc., P.O. Box 837, Kihei, HI 96753-0837

© 1992, 1994, 1998 by Anonymous.

This Paradise Research Publications Edition is published by arrangement with Good Book Publishing Company, P.O. Box 837, Kihei, Maui, HI 96753-0837

Cover Design: Lili Crawford (Maui Cyber Design)

The publication of this volume does not imply affiliation with, nor approval nor endorsement from, Alcoholics Anonymous World Services, Inc.

Publisher's Cataloging in Publication

B., Dick.
   Dr. Bob and his library : a Major A.A. Spiritual Source /
Dick B. -- 3rd ed.
   p. cm.
   Includes index and appendices
   ISBN: 1-885803-25-7
   1. Smith, Robert Holbrook, 1879-1950--Library--Catalogs.
   2. Bibliography--Best books--Theology. 3. Theology--Catalogs.
   I. Title.
Z7755.B53 1994   230'.092'016

(previously published by Paradise Research Publications, Inc., ISBN: 1-885803-00-1; Good Book Publishing Company, ISBN: 1-881212-00-9; and The Bishop of Books, ISBN: 1-877686-04-2; previous title: Dr. Bob's Library: An AA-Good Book Connection)

Library of Congress Catalog Card Number: 98-92130

To Danny and Denise W., & the A.A. Roots Revival Group

Study to shew thyself approved unto God, a workman that needeth not to be ashamed, rightly dividing the word of truth.

2 Timothy 2:15

Contents

Foreword to First Edition

At a time when Alcoholics Anonymous seems to be "changing," some call for a return to "basics." But of course that is impossible. We cannot go back to the past. *Basics* that are called "basics" will never be the same as understandings implicitly assumed because they are shared by all. And so the question becomes: Is there any middle between the impossible attempt to recapture the past and the mindless rejection of our own origins? Of course there is. We can learn from the past.

Dick B.'s dedicated efforts will make this possible for a new generation of Alcoholics Anonymous. Reading was important in early A.A. Early issues of *The A.A. Grapevine* carried lengthy book reviews. Works recommended ranged from Santayana's *The Idea of Christ in the Gospels* to *The Mussorgsky Reader*, from *Great Adventures and Explorations* to Strecker's *Fundamentals of Psychology*. Meanwhile, in the Midwest and other areas where A.A.'s Oxford Group ties lasted longer and where Dr. Bob Smith's influence predominated, a different kind of reading was emphasized. The reading program that came out of early Akron A.A. focused on inspirational religious literature; much of it in fact consisted of works that members first met within the Oxford Group.

Nothing, of course, differs more than taste—certainly in reading, especially over time, particularly among alcoholics, and most surely in matters of "the spiritual." Yet even if most spiritual literature travels poorly over time, there are always classics buried in any list, in any generation. The problem that is our opportunity lies in this: each reader must find his or her own "classics"—those works that in some mysterious way uniquely "speak to the condition" of each individual, to where he or she is *today*. But how to find such readings? For members of Alcoholics Anonymous, the library of Dr. Robert Holbrook Smith would seem a good place to begin the search.

For such searches are again underway. As recognition grows that A.A. is not "treatment" but a *spiritual way of life*, both members and students of Alcoholics Anonymous are rediscovering how important reading material was to the fellowship's first members, to those who formulated its program. The treatment people and some researchers call such reading "bibliotherapy," and they tend to interpret it through that psychological lens. A more classic vocabulary, one truer to A.A.'s own story, would term it "spiritual reading." According to the twelfth-century author of the *Ladder of Monks*, the spiritual exercise of reading precedes meditation and even prayer: readings furnish the mind, readying and honing it for those Eleventh-Step practices.

We can be grateful to Dick B. for his diligent work, which makes available to us not a mere listing of books, but a sense of how they were read and a summary of what they contain. Dick's careful and thorough research, the details of which he generously shares with us, brings his own spirituality to bear on the task of understanding the spirituality of the Akronites among the first generation of Alcoholics Anonymous. His has been a labor of love, and even readers who disagree with some of Dick's assumptions and enthusiasms cannot help but be impressed by—and grateful for—both his labor and his love.

ERNEST KURTZ, Ph.D.
Author of *Not-God: A History of Alcoholics Anonymous*

Preface to the Third Edition

Upon completion of our thirteenth title on the spiritual history of early Alcoholics Anonymous, we found a new look at Dr. Bob's library was much needed. For one thing, Dr. Bob's children had unearthed and made available to the author for inspection a number of additional books their father read and circulated. These included not only several books on Christian prayer and healing, but also some early treasures, such as the first book by Professor Henry Drummond, who was a favorite of Dr. Bob's. Also, we have become fairly certain that Dr. Bob had no "required reading list." Several early AAs indicated Dr. Bob did not push his reading on anyone. His daughter told the author Dr. Bob had no "required" reading. People sought him out for suggested reading. And, in addition to the Bible, there were a good many books he strongly recommended.

Dr. Bob said he had read an immense number of books recommended by the Oxford Group people. Since the writing of the first edition of *Dr. Bob's Library*, the author has learned of many Oxford Group and Sam Shoemaker books of the 1920s and 1930s that were widely known and therefore quite probably read not only by Dr. Bob, but also by his wife (Anne), Henrietta Seiberling (an early co-founder), and T. Henry and Clarace Williams (two other early co-founders). We now know there was a large collection of Oxford Group, Shoemaker, and other Christian literature present at the early A.A. meetings in the home of T. Henry and Clarace Williams, and that the books were used by those present at those early Akron meetings.

The new information about Oxford Group-Shoemaker-Christian literature of the 1920s and 1930s has come first from the host of Oxford Group-Moral Re-Armament people with whom the author has conversed and corresponded over the past eight years. In addition, the rector and the vicar at Calvary Church in New York (Sam Shoemaker's church) each generously opened the doors to the author. And in late 1993, the author learned of a large number of Oxford Group books (other than those previously listed) that were recommended by Calvary Church's parish publication, *The Calvary Evangel*, in A.A.'s formative period between 1935 and 1939. They were stocked in the parish's bookstore and were widely distributed in America. Even more were discovered among the fifty-eight boxes the author and his son searched at The Episcopal Church Archives in Austin, Texas.

Our research has also recently disclosed a good deal of new evidence from the lips of Bill Wilson as to what he learned about the Bible in early Akron days. Also as to what his early fellow-AAs studied in the Bible during that period. Since A.A.'s Bible focus in the early days centered in Akron, where Dr. Bob was the leader, his collection of books sheds new light on the Biblical language and ideas Bill Wilson included in the Big Book. Also, we have learned how the information gained by Dr. Bob and his wife was probably disseminated to early AAs and their families at Dr. Bob's home. This has enabled us to piece together a clearer picture of what Dr. Bob taught the more than 5,000 alcoholics he helped, and how he actually applied to their needs the vast amount of information he gleaned from the Bible and the other books he read.

Acknowledgements

Many have helped inspire and construct this work.

At the personal level, my son, Ken, is first in my mind. His deep love for God, and the accuracy and integrity of His Word, gave me a purpose in this effort. On the practical side, Ken is a fine scholar, Bible student, and very knowledgeable in the computer field. He encouraged my research work and the purchase of a computer. He has fielded innumerable calls and given much assistance at all levels as the work progressed.

A.A.'s former Archivist, Frank M., in New York, was tops on the firing line of supporters. Bill Pittman provided information and help from his large reservoir of writings on the history of A.A., the Oxford Group, and Reverend Sam Shoemaker.

Our work would have come to nothing without the complete cooperation and support of Dr. Bob's children. They have responded to many requests and phone calls for information. So have the Seiberlings—former Congressman John and his sisters Dorothy Seiberling and Mary Seiberling Huhn—concerning their mother's contribution to A.A. Later, Dorothy Williams Culver (the daughter of T. Henry Williams) joined the group of providers and gave much help.

Oxford Group leaders and activists have been immensely helpful. These include the Rev. Harry Almond, Kenneth Belden, Terry Blair, the Rev. Howard Blake, Sydney Cook, Charles Haines, Mrs. W. Irving Harris, Michael Henderson, James Houck, the Rev. T. Willard Hunter, Michael Hutchinson, Donald Johnson, Garth Lean, Dr. Morris Martin, James D. and Eleanor F. Newton,

Richard Ruffin, L. Parks Shipley, Sr., George Vondermuhll, Jr., and Ted Watt. Over the past year, the daughters of the Reverend Canon Samuel M. Shoemaker, Jr., have opened entirely new vistas as to how Sam Shoemaker (a major American Oxford Group leader and writer) impacted on early A.A., including its entire Akron genesis. Shoemaker's daughters are Canon Sally Shoemaker Robinson and Helen ("Nickie") Shoemaker Haggart.

Others who have been of much help include A.A. historian and scholar, Dr. Ernest Kurtz; A.A.'s first archivist, Nell Wing; Ray G., archivist at Dr. Bob's home; Gail L., Founders Day archivist; and Paul L., archivist at Bill W.'s home at Stepping Stones. So, too, Mel B. of Toledo, author of *New Wine: The Spiritual Roots of the Twelve Step Miracle*; Dennis C., who has provided much material originally owned by Bill and Lois Wilson; Mitch K., who is working on the Clarence Snyder story; and Bruce W.

There are others, including men I sponsor in A.A., and the members of my Bible fellowship, who have lent continued interest and support. Special mention goes to my Bible fellowship friend and helper, Patrick Burry of Maui. Thanks, too, to my own sponsor in A.A., Henry B., who encouraged me to continue this work for a long time to come.

Finally, this work could not have been produced without the help of the San Francisco Theological Seminary Library, the Golden Gate Baptist Seminary Library, the Hartford Seminary Archives, Princeton University Libraries, the Graduate Theological Union Libraries in the San Francisco Bay Area, and the libraries at the University of Akron.

1

The Story of Doctor Bob's Reading

Doctor Bob was an alcoholic; an Akron, Ohio, physician; and a co-founder of Alcoholics Anonymous. He met A.A.'s other co-founder, Bill W., on Mother's Day, 1935. Together they practiced the spiritual program they jointly developed.

Dr. Bob was able to stay sober for the remaining fifteen years of his life and personally to help more than 5,000 alcoholics in their recovery. His full name and title were Robert Holbrook Smith, M.D. And this is a brief account of the vast amount of reading he did in the Bible–which he affectionately called "The Good Book"–and in a large number of spiritual books which dealt primarily with the Bible and Christianity.

We will include some of the comments Dr. Bob made as to where A.A. got its basic ideas. Also, a great deal of information–never, to our knowledge, presented before–about precisely what Dr. Bob studied as he made his contributions to A.A.'s ideas.

This book will be more than an annotated bibliography. It should enable the reader to see at a glance the spiritual subjects to which Dr. Bob's attention was directed. It will also highlight for the reader certain areas to pursue for spiritual growth and understanding, applying the same tools that Dr. Bob used so successfully with the many alcoholics he helped in Ohio.

Dr. Bob was born August 8, 1879. In A.A.'s official biography of him, Dr. Bob's religious up-bringing is dismissed with this brief statement made at some point by Dr. Bob himself:

> From childhood through high school, I was more or less forced to go to church, Sunday school and evening service, Monday-night Christian Endeavor, and sometimes to Wednesday-evening prayer meeting. . . . This had the effect of making me resolve that when I was free from parental domination, I would never again darken the doors of a church.[1]

Adding to this quote, the A.A. biography states, "Dr. Bob kept his resolution 'steadfastly' for the next forty years, except when circumstances made it unwise" (p. 12). And this tiny addendum reflects a common belief the author has heard in A.A. that Dr. Bob was somehow hostile to church and to religious growth through a church.[2] Yet those do not appear to be the facts.

In his last major talk to A.A., in December of 1948, Dr. Bob himself discussed his religious background and Bill's, and said as to his own religious training as a youth:

> Now the interesting part of all this is not the sordid details, but the situation that we two fellows were in. We had both been associated with the Oxford Group, Bill in New York, for five months, and I in Akron, for two and a half years. Bill had acquired their idea of service. I had not, but I had done *an immense amount of reading they had recommended*. I had *refreshed my memory of the Good Book*, and I had *had excellent training in that as a youngster* (emphasis added).[3]

---

[1] *DR. BOB and the Good Oldtimers* (New York: Alcoholics Anonymous World Services, Inc., 1980), p. 12.

[2] But see Bob Smith, *Children of the Healer* (IL: Parkside, 1992), p. 127; Cf. Shem and Surrey, *Bill W. and Dr. Bob* (NY: Samuel French, 1987), pp. 8, 59.

[3] *The Co-Founders of Alcoholics Anonymous: Biographical sketches, Their Last Major Talks* (New York: Alcoholics Anonymous World Services, Inc., 1972, 1975), p. 7.

These are not the remarks of one who was spurning his youthful, religious training in church. On the contrary, Dr. Bob appeared, at a later and more mature point in his life, to realize just how valuable his religious upbringing had been. We therefore investigated what Dr. Bob *did* do in the church category. See Appendix 1 for full details.

Our research showed Dr. Bob and his wife, Anne, were charter members of the Westminster United Presbyterian Church in Akron, Ohio, from June 3, 1936, to April 3, 1942. And, later, before his death, he became a communicant at St. Paul's Episcopal Church in Akron.

Dr. Bob said his early religious training was substantial, and that he was grateful for it. But the real point is that Dr. Bob met Bill W., his stockbroker acquaintance, bringing with him some very substantial and valuable spiritual assets from his childhood.[4]

Bill, by contrast, had no such significant background or training. He was "head of the Y.M.C.A." in high school. But his biographer added, "As a student, if he'd had any God, it had been the God of Science, of facts."[5] A.A. historian, Dr. Ernest Kurtz, wrote, "Of Bill's earlier exposure to religion, little is known—probably because there is little to know. . . . [Y]oung Bill Wilson had 'left the church' at about twelve—on a 'matter of principle.' . . . Bill's recollections revealed that the young Wilson had no 'religion' beyond an adolescent romanticism."[6] Bill himself completed a questionnaire in early A.A. before the Big Book was published, and said he had briefly tried Christian Science and "Metaphysics" but found them ineffective for him.[7]

---

[4] See Appendix 1.

[5] Robert Thomsen, *Bill W.* (New York: Harper & Row, 1975), pp. 57, 213.

[6] Ernest Kurtz, *Not-God: A History of Alcoholics Anonymous*, expanded ed. (MN: Hazelden, 1991), p. 16.

[7] Wilson and a number of early AAs completed individual questionnaires on a number of subjects, including their religious backgrounds. The statements are on file in A.A. Archives in New York. See also, *Pass It On* (New York: Alcoholics Anonymous World Services, Inc., 1984), pp. 230-31; and Bill Pittman, *AA The Way It Began* (Seattle, Glen Abbey Books, 1988), p. 150.

In any event, there was a spiritual renewal in Dr. Bob's life, beginning at least as early as January of 1933.[8] In 1931, a "miracle" had occurred on a train near Denver, Colorado. It involved tire manufacturer Harvey Firestone's son, Russell (Bud), who was an alcoholic. James Newton, an Oxford Group member and a Firestone assistant, prevailed upon Bud, the alcoholic, to go with him to an Episcopal Bishops' conference in Denver. Newton put Bud Firestone in touch with the Rev. Sam Shoemaker, an American Oxford Group leader, who was Rector of the Calvary Episcopal Church in New York. On his return train trip, Sam Shoemaker helped young Bud Firestone make a decision for Christ. Thereafter, Bud applied in his life the principles and practices of "A First Century Christian Fellowship" (also known as "the Oxford Group"). As a consequence, he maintained sobriety for a substantial period of time. The family doctor called the transformation a medical miracle.

Harvey Firestone was so grateful for his son's deliverance that he invited Oxford Group Founder, Dr. Frank Buchman, and a team of thirty to conduct a ten-day campaign in Akron. Oxford Group team members from the United States and Europe, including Buchman, Olive Jones (an author, a teacher, and superintendent at Calvary Church in New York), Jim Newton, and H. Kenaston Twitchell (Dr. Shoemaker's brother-in-law) all filled pulpits at Protestant Churches in the Akron area.

Meetings were held throughout the day, and they culminated in a dinner for 1,200 prominent citizens of the community. The events made headlines. Henrietta Seiberling, Anne Ripley Smith (Dr. Bob's wife), and their friends, Clarace Williams and Delphine

---

[8] The information that follows concerning the Oxford Group events in Akron, Ohio, in January of 1933 is taken from these sources: (1) James Newton, *Uncommon Friends* (New York: Harcourt Brace Jovanovich, Publishers, 1988), pp. 83-88; (2) Garth Lean, *On The Tail of a Comet* (Colorado Springs: Helmers & Howard, 1988), pp. 151-52; (3) *Pass It On*, p. 141; (4) *DR. BOB*, p. 55; and (5) For a comprehensive study, see Dick B., *The Akron Genesis of Alcoholics Anonymous*, 2d ed. (Kihei, HI: Paradise Research Publications, 1998), pp. 17-51.

Weber, were at the Oxford Group meetings.[9] At once, they "joined" the Oxford Group and its Biblically-oriented program. Dr. Bob himself soon followed their lead, still later attending Oxford Group meetings on Wednesdays at T. Henry Williams' Akron home.

And Dr. Bob began—though drinking much during the period—a two-and-a-half year spiritual renewal of that which he had begun in his intense childhood training. *DR. BOB and the Good Oldtimers* records: "At this time, he began his conscious search for truth through a concentrated study of the Bible over two-and-one-half years before his meeting with Bill" (p. 306). Once again, this brief quote does not convey the whole story of Dr. Bob's spiritual quest in the two-and-one-half year period, nor thereafter.

When Bill W. first met Dr. Bob in Akron on Mother's Day of 1935 and had his almost six hour discussion with Dr. Bob, Bill was "alive" with answers to Dr. Bob's drinking problem. But such sharing as Bill did from his six months of experience with the Oxford Group in New York, was hardly equal to Dr. Bob's spiritual knowledge at the time. *DR. BOB and the Good Oldtimers* indicated Dr. Bob was much more impressed with the fact that another alcoholic was telling him, than with what Bill actually said. Dr. Bob said "that, although it was helpful, he had heard most of it before" (p. 69).

---

[9] On June 8, 1991, Sue Smith Windows provided the author with a signed statement which says of the Oxford Group meetings in 1933, "My mother, Anne, was at that first meeting with Clarace Williams, Henrietta Seiberling, and Delphine Weber, the wife of the superintendent of King School." There are some interesting facts about Mrs. Smith's three companions: (1) The subsequent Wednesday night Oxford Group meetings—which were regularly attended by Dr. Bob, Anne, and the "alcoholic squad of the Oxford Group"—were held at Clarace Williams's home. (2) Henrietta Seiberling was a leader and "called the shots" at these meetings. (3) The meetings were later moved to King School where Delphine Weber's husband was superintendent. The King School Group became A.A.'s first group, was attended by Dr. Bob and Anne, and still exists today though its meeting place has moved to another location. All these points are covered in the Windows statement of 6/8/91.

RHS, the memorial article written at the time of Dr. Bob's death, said of the 1933-1935 period of Bob's attendance at the Oxford Group:

> Anne became deeply interested in the group and her interest sustained Dr. Bob's. He delved into religious philosophy, he read the Scriptures, he studied spiritual interpretations, the lives of the Saints. Like a sponge he soaked up the spiritual philosophies of the ages.[10]

At another point, it added:

> For the next two and a half years, Bob attended Oxford Group meetings regularly and gave much time and study to its philosophy. . . . "I read everything I could find, and talked to everyone who I thought knew anything about it," Dr. Bob said. He read the Scriptures, studied the lives of the saints, and did what he could to soak up the spiritual and religious philosophies of the ages (p. 56).

The pamphlet, *Co-Founders*, said that in the early thirties, Dr. Bob, in a desperate search for an answer to his problem, began to attend meetings of the Oxford Group, feeling he could benefit from its philosophy and other spiritual teachings.[11]

Not-God records of Bill's first three weeks of living with Dr. Bob and Anne Smith that:

> Bill Wilson found himself in awe of Dr. Bob's "spiritual knowledge" and cherished the guidance of Anne Smith as each morning her pleasant voice read and interpreted the Christian Scriptures and the Oxford Group devotional books (p. 32).[12]

---

[10] *RHS* (New York: A.A. Grapevine, Inc., 1951), p. 21.

[11] *The Co-Founders of Alcoholics Anonymous*, p. 4.

[12] This statement does not present an accurate picture of the books Anne Smith read and interpreted to Bill Wilson, Dr. Bob, and many others. Anne read from the entire

(continued...)

And it was at this point—at the home of Dr. Bob and Anne Smith—that the assembling of the specific, basic A.A. ideas began in earnest.

Dr. Bob and Bill sat up for hours each night for three months sharing the ideas they had.[13] As pointed out above, Anne read extensively from the Bible and a great many Christian books, including those of the Oxford Group. Henrietta Seiberling was an avid Bible student, an Oxford Group member, and one of Dr. Bob's most inspired teachers. Her son, John F. Seiberling, informed the author that Henrietta had read *all* the Oxford Group books of the 1930's.[14] We also know now the large number of *other* Christian books she read, a reading list that approached Dr. Bob's in scope.[15]

Not-God states there were almost daily visits at the Smith home in the summer of 1935 during which "Henrietta Seiberling provided their spiritual nourishment and much religious education" (p. 40). Dr. Bob and Bill attended weekly Oxford Group meetings at the T. Henry Williams home together.[16] Henrietta was the leader at many of these weekly Oxford Group meetings.[17] She wrote, "Every Wednesday night, I would speak on some new experience or spiritual idea I had read."[18]

---

[12] (...continued)
Bible and from a vast number of Christian books and pamphlets, not merely those which were "Oxford Group devotional books." See Dick B., *Anne Smith's Journal, 1933-1939* (Kihei, HI: Paradise Research Publications, 1994); and *The Akron Genesis*, pp. 55-64, 111-12, 337-48.

[13] *DR. BOB*, p. 97.

[14] Letter to the author from former Congressman John F. Seiberling, dated July 5, 1991.

[15] See Dick B., *The Akron Genesis*, pp. 107-123.

[16] Kurtz, *Not-God*, p. 40.

[17] *DR. BOB*, pp. 156-57.

[18] Henrietta B. Seiberling, *Origins of Alcoholics Anonymous* (A transcript of remarks by Henrietta B. Seiberling: Transcript prepared by Congressman John F. Seiberling of a telephone conversation with his mother, Henrietta, in the spring of 1971) *Employee Assistance Quarterly*, 1985 (1), pp. 33-39. The author has a copy of this transcript in his possession.

Bill and Dr. Bob shared Quiet Time in the morning with Anne. According to Ernest Kurtz, her "guided" Bible readings certainly covered two themes: Paul to the Corinthians on love and the Apostle James on the crucial importance of works if faith were to have meaning.[19] Sue Smith Windows, Dr. Bob's daughter, informed the author that Anne often talked at length on spiritual subjects with Bill when Dr. Bob was not present.[20] During this entire period, Anne Smith was compiling her journal, covering the Biblical, Christian, and religious subjects and books she was studying.[21] Later, most of that journal was typed up for her by her daughter, Sue.[22] The author has carefully scrutinized Anne's Journal—including the many spiritual books and pamphlets that Anne had read and recommended in that Journal. Sue wrote the author that her father had read all the books and pamphlets Anne mentioned in her Journal.[23]

There are many facts concerning Dr. Bob's reading during this early period that deserve attention. Several of the facts were provided by Dr. Bob himself. Dr. Bob said:

----

[19] Kurtz, *Not-God*, p. 40.

[20] Telephone interview by author with Sue Windows, December, 1991.

[21] At the request of Sue Smith Windows, A.A. Archives in New York accorded the author the courtesy of a complete copy of a sixty-four-page manuscript, partially typed and partially written in Anne Smith's own hand. Some, including Dr. Ernest Kurtz, have called the manuscript Anne Smith's Oxford Group Workbook (See *Not-God*, p. 331, note 32). The author was able to inspect an additional copy of the manuscript during a visit to Bill Wilson's home at Stepping Stones in Bedford Hills, New York, in October of 1991. We have chosen to call the manuscript *Anne Smith's Journal* because it comprehends more than just Oxford Group materials. For example, it mentions, discusses, and recommends the reading of a number of books by authors who were not connected with the Oxford Group, and it discusses several Bible chapters and verses not particularly emphasized in Oxford Group writings the author has examined. All further references to this work are in the text as "Journal."

[22] Sue Smith Windows informed the author in Akron, Ohio, during a lengthy interview in June, 1991, that she had typed her mother's Journal pages while she (Sue) was at business college. On August 9, 1991, Sue wrote she believed she had typed the Journal pages in 1937 or 1938 and that Anne was in the process of compiling her Journal from about 1933 to 1939.

[23] Letter from Sue Windows to the author, dated August 9, 1991.

1. "[T]hey [the early AAs] were convinced that the answer to their problems was in the Good Book. To some of us older ones, the parts we found absolutely essential were the Sermon on the Mount, the 13th chapter of First Corinthians, and the Book of James."[24]

2. "I didn't write the Twelve Steps. I had nothing to do with the writing of them. But I think I probably had something to do with them indirectly. . . . There was hardly a night [during the three months of Bill's stay in the summer of 1935] that we didn't sit up until two or three o'clock, talking. It would be hard for me to say that, during these nightly discussions around our kitchen table, nothing was said that influenced the writing of the Twelve Steps. We already had the basic ideas, though not in terse and tangible form. We got them . . . as a result of our study of the Good Book."[25]

Dr. Bob said "the Sermon on the Mount . . . [contained] the underlying spiritual philosophy of A.A."[26] Also, in his last major address to A.A., he said:

The four absolutes [of the Oxford Group], as we called them, were the only yardsticks we had in the early days, before the Steps. I think the absolutes still hold good and can be extremely helpful. . . . Almost always, if I measure my decision carefully by the yardsticks of absolute honesty, absolute unselfishness, absolute purity, and absolute love, and it checks up pretty well with those four, then my answer can't be very far out of the way.[27]

---

[24] *DR. BOB*, p. 96.

[25] *DR. BOB*, pp. 96-97.

[26] *DR. BOB*, pp. 228. Also, A.A. historian Mel B. informed the author in a telephone conversation that Bill Wilson had several times told him (Mel B.) that the Sermon on the Mount contained the underlying spiritual philosophy of A.A.

[27] *The Co-Founders of Alcoholics Anonymous*, pp. 12-13. These four absolutes were reconstructed by Dr. Robert E. Speer from the teachings of Jesus, expanded upon by Dr. Henry Wright with other verses from the New Testament, and adopted by Dr. Frank

(continued...)

The bottom line in this period is described as follows in *DR. BOB and the Good Oldtimers*:

> This was the beginning of A.A.'s 'flying blind period.' They had the Bible, and they had the precepts of the Oxford Group. . . . They were working, or working out, the A.A. program—the Twelve Steps—without quite knowing how they were doing it (p. 96).

Bill later made an unusual statement many years after this so-called "flying blind period." Bill indicated to A.A. co-founders, T. Henry and Clarace Williams, just how much he had learned about the Bible from his stay with Dr. Bob and Anne in the summer of 1935 and from his later associations with "the alcoholic squad of the Oxford Group" in Akron. Bill said:

> I learned a great deal from you people [T. Henry and Clarace Williams], from the Smiths themselves, and from Henrietta [Seiberling]. I hadn't looked in the Bible, up to this time, at all. You see, I had the . . . [conversion] experience first and then this rushing around to help drunks and nothing happened.[28]

A little-remembered remark Bill Wilson made in his lecture at Yale University Summer School of Alcohol Studies, on August 3, 1944, also bears on the subject of early A.A. reading. Bill said:

---

[27] (...continued)
Buchman as the standards of the Oxford Group. See Lean, *On The Tail of A Comet*, pp. 76-77; The Layman with a Notebook, *What Is The Oxford Group?* (London: Oxford University Press, 1933), pp. 7-8, 74-117. For a thorough study, see Dick B., *The Oxford Group & Alcoholics Anonymous*, 2d ed. (Kihei, HI: Paradise Research Publications, 1998), pp. 237-46.

[28] The author unearthed this humble and candid statement by Bill Wilson as he reviewed a transcript of Bill Wilson's taped interview with T. Henry and Clarace Williams. The tape was made on December 12, 1954. The author inspected the transcript at A.A. General Service Archives in New York.

For a great many of us have taken to reading the Bible. It could not have been presented at first, but sooner or later in his second, third, or fourth year, the A.A. will be found reading his Bible quite as often—or more—as he will a standard psychological work.[29]

DR. BOB and the Good Oldtimers elaborated further:

The Bible was stressed as reading material, of course (p. 151).

We had much prayer together in those days and began quietly to read Scripture and discuss a practical approach to its application to our lives (p. 111).

Morning quiet time continued to be an important part of the recovery program in 1938-39, as did the spiritual reading from which the early members derived a good deal of their inspiration (p. 150).

Of the Wednesday meeting in Akron, "Usually, the person who led the Wednesday meeting took something from *The Upper Room* or some other literature as a subject. Sometimes, they selected a theme such as 'My Utmost Effort' or 'My Highest Goal.' There

---

[29] W.W., "The Fellowship of Alcoholics Anonymous," Lecture 29 in *Alcohol, Science and Society: Twenty-Nine Lectures with Discussions As Given at the Yale Summer School of Alcohol Studies* (New Haven: Quarterly Journal of Studies on Alcohol, 1945), p. 467. In this same lecture, Bill illustrated the impact of the Bible on A.A. by telling the story of how A.A.'s best-known and avowed atheist, Jimmy B., got sober. Bill told how Jimmy kept getting drunk and finally showed up at Bill's office asking about prayer and meditation. Bill said Jimmy had told about his experience in a little second rate hotel where he had nearly died from the worst seizure he had ever had, and that something in him had "given way." Bill said, "He [Jimmy] had thought to himself, 'Maybe these fellas have got something with their God-business.' His hand reached out, in the darkness, and touched something in his bureau. It was a Gideon Bible. Jimmy picked it up and he read from it. I do not know just what he read, and I have always had a queer reluctance to ask him. But Jimmy has not had a drink to this day, and that was about 5 years ago" (p. 468).

would be a Quiet Time. Then different people would tell something out of their own experience" (p. 139).[30]

In his report to John D. Rockefeller, Jr., on the nature of the successful Akron program, Frank Amos covered two points important for our book: (1) In describing the program, he said of the alcoholic, "He must have devotions every morning—a 'quiet time' of prayer and some reading from the Bible and other religious literature. Unless this is faithfully followed, there is grave danger of backsliding."[31] (2) *DR BOB* said of the Amos report, "Stressing Dr. Bob's importance in the work at Akron, Frank Amos went on to note that even though there were other able men in the group, they all looked to Dr. Bob for leadership."[32]

One early researcher claimed that Dr. Bob had a "Required Reading List."[33] The Bible tops that list, but only three other books, and a periodical, are named.[34] Our research shows, however, that Dr. Bob strongly recommended a large number of other books in addition to the four on the so-called "Required"

---

[30] *The Upper Room: Daily Devotions for Family and Individual Use* (Nashville, Tennessee: Issued quarterly by the General Committee on Evangelism through the Department of Home Missions, Evangelism, Hospitals, Board of Missions, Methodist Episcopal Church, South). The first quarterly was issued for the months of April, May, June, 1935. The author has a copy of this first quarterly issue, and also has recently been provided by the managing editor of *The Upper Room* with copies of almost every quarterly printed during the formative years from 1935 to 1939. According to Sue Smith Windows, copies of *The Upper Room* were brought either to her home or to the Wednesday Oxford Group meetings by her mother-in-law, Lucy Galbraith. Sue's first husband, Ernie Galbraith, was an alcoholic who attended the Oxford Group meetings at the Williams home.

[31] *DR. BOB*, p. 131.

[32] *DR BOB*, p. 131

[33] Pittman, *AA The Way It Began*, p. 197.

[34] In *AA The Way It Began*, at page 197, that author described "Dr. Bob's 'Required Reading List,'" as follows: (1) The Holy Bible, King James Version - The Sermon on the Mount, The Lord's Prayer, The Book of James, The 13th Chapter of First Corinthians. (2) *The Upper Room* (Methodist periodical). (3) *The Greatest Thing in the World*—Henry Drummond. (4) *The Varieties of Religious Experience*—William James. (5) *For Sinners Only*—A. J. Russell.

list. Also, that his "favorites" included a host of books by Glenn Clark, E. Stanley Jones, Emmet Fox, and James Allen that are not mentioned. Furthermore, Dr. Bob's daughter, Sue, told the author that Dr. Bob never "required" *any* reading. Dr. Bob himself was a voracious reader and always stressed the Bible, or the "Good Book," as he called it, as the place to find the answers.[35]

Hospitalization was a must in the early days of Akron A.A., and *DR. BOB and the Good Oldtimers* states, "These patients were allowed only a Bible as reading material" (p. 102). As we shall see shortly, daily Bible devotionals were regular fare in early A.A. And the books that Dr. Bob owned, read, recommended, and often loaned out were about the Bible and Biblical subjects. Examples are Henry Drummond's study of 1 Corinthians 13, Oswald Chambers's study of the Sermon on the Mount, and the Oxford Group books on a wide variety of Biblical principles.[36]

And now we turn to what has not been done. To our knowledge, there has been no study of the names, the content, or the quantity of the Biblical, religious, and spiritual books which Dr. Bob did read and study so intensely.

We know the quantity of books was large. Dr. Bob often said to his son, "Smitty," "Well, I should know something, I've read for at least an hour every night of my adult life—drunk or sober."[37] And Dr. Bob's daughter, Sue, recalled to the author that her father frequently stayed up late into the night studying the Bible.[38]

---

[35] Dr. Bob's son, Robert Smith, wrote the author in November, 1991, that his father was "a voracious reader." For Dr. Bob's own words, see *DR. BOB*, p. 96. See also the account which Clarence S. gave to his wife, Grace: Dick B., *That Amazing Grace: The Role of Clarence and Grace S. in Alcoholics Anonymous* (San Rafael, CA: Paradise Research Publications, 1996), p. 31.

[36] See Sherwood Sunderland Day, *The Principles of the Oxford Group* (Pamphlet published by the Oxford Group and printed in Great Britain at the University Press, Oxford, by John Johnson, printer to the University, no date). Day says on page 3, "The principles of 'The Oxford Group' are the principles of the Bible."

[37] *RHS*, pp. 35-36.

[38] Interview with Sue Smith Windows, Akron, Ohio, June, 1991.

DR. BOB and the Good Oldtimers added these facts: (1) Emma K. was a close friend of the Smiths. She attended to Anne Smith during her last years, and—with her husband, Lavelle—lived with Dr. Bob for the year and a half of his life after Anne died. Emma said, "He read everything. I wish you could have seen the books" (p. 309). (2) Dr. Bob's son, Smitty, said, "He read about every religion . . . not only the Christian religion. He could tell you about the Koran, Confucius, even voodooism, and many other things. He read the Bible from cover to cover three times and could quote favorite verses verbatim" (p. 310). (3) According to Paul S., "Dr. Bob's morning devotion consisted of a short prayer, a 20-minute study of a familiar verse from the Bible, and a quiet period of waiting for directions as to where he, that day, should find use for his talent" (p. 314).

So we come to the matter of what Dr. Bob *did* read. The sheer quantity of his books seems to have overwhelmed those who reported on his reading.

Dorothy S. M. recalled for Bill W. Dr. Bob's "pile of books . . . stacks by his bed and under his bed and everywhere else."[39] She mentioned Emmet Fox's *The Sermon on the Mount*, Henry Drummond's *The Greatest Thing in the World*, and *The Upper Room*. Then she added, "Bob went on to explore every type of philosophy and religion. . . . If people asked, he'd tell them, but he didn't push books at people."[40]

Ernie G. of Toledo recalled that Dr. Bob and his wife, Anne, did "share books and things" when Ernie's wife, Ruth, was "getting a spiritual answer"—"trying to get a spiritual healing" for an illness.[41] As we said, Emma K. remarked that Dr. Bob had read "everything" and commented on the quantity of his books. Dr. Bob's son, Smitty, said Dr. Bob read about every religion. He added, citing *Tertium Organum* as an example, "I tried to read some of his books and couldn't understand them." A.A.'s official

---

[39] *DR. BOB*, p. 309.

[40] See Dorothy S. M.'s comments, reported in *DR. BOB*, pp. 310-11.

[41] *DR. BOB*, pp. 312-13.

biography, *DR. BOB*, lists "some others" Smitty mentioned.[42]
But only nine were specified.

Bill Wilson was, as we have stated, simply "in awe" of Dr.
Bob's knowledge. He said, "Bob was far ahead of me in that sort
of activity" [the spiritual, prayer realm].[43]

It was with this tiny bit of information about "stacks"—a "pile
of books," about "every religion"—that we started this quest to
learn the full extent of Dr. Bob's reading. We felt, and now know,
that history should record the precise nature and contents of Dr.
Bob's library. Dr. Bob studied a great deal about the Bible and
other spiritual subjects—particularly for a man who was neither a
lifetime church-goer, nor a professed Bible student. He read with
a purpose—to learn more about the Good Book and other spiritual
matters. And he applied what he read. His reading—from 1933 to
the end of his life—was directed toward helping himself and
thousands of others in their quest to overcome alcoholism. And
Dr. Bob's studies and service bore fruit.

The success that was to put early A.A. on the map was in
Akron, Ohio; and, as Frank Amos reported to John D.
Rockefeller, Jr., it was a success which there was attributed to Dr.
Bob's leadership—and, necessarily, to the information he had spent
so much time acquiring.[44] These statements do not detract one bit

---

[42] *DR. BOB*, p. 310.

[43] *DR. BOB*, p. 315.

[44] *DR. BOB* quotes a letter from Bill W., which stated, "Dr. Smith has had more
experience and has obtained better results than anyone else" (p. 174). *Pass It On*, A.A.'s
official biography of Bill Wilson, states these things: (1) "There is certainly no denying
that in the first few years, A.A. grew more rapidly in Akron than it did in New York,
and there were those who attributed the success to Dr. Bob's strong leadership" (p. 157).
(2) "While Lois [Bill Wilson's wife] also later admitted that their success rate was low
during the 1935-1936 period at Clinton Street [in New York], she pointed out that many
of the alcoholics Bill worked with during that time did recover later on" (p. 166). (3)
"The Amos report showed just how much Dr. Bob and his fellow members had accomplished in the not-quite-three years since that first meeting with Bill. It stated that there
were now 50 men and two women who had been 'reformed,' and it emphasized Dr.
Bob's all-important role as leader" (p. 187). See also Kurtz, *Not-God*, pp. 43, 58, 62,
note 58 on p. 230.

from the flare that A.A.'s other co-founder, Bill Wilson, had for writing, speaking, assimilating, organizing, promoting, and structuring. It was undoubtedly Bill's organizing genius and dedicated work that were responsible for much of A.A.'s growth from a mere 100—mostly in the Akron-Cleveland area—to today's massive numbers close to 2 million. But Bill himself never once minimized Dr. Bob's spiritual knowledge or contribution.

We do not want to present a dry list of some 150 books that Dr. Bob studied and favored. Such a list would do little to attract either readers or study. Even to categorize the books does some damage to the fact that most covered *many* subjects pertaining to the Bible and Christianity. And, if placed in a particular niche, a book might not be read due to disinterest in the niche, whereas the author found so many of these books to be captivating, informative, and helpful in their totality. So we will simply start with the sources that establish what the books were, and then do our best to put the reading matter in a manageable and interesting form, with the hope that our readers will themselves pick up the challenge, open to this or that book, and see the immensely important literature that A.A.'s co-founder studied.

We believe A.A.'s spiritual sources were pinpointed by Dr. Bob and by Bill Wilson. The viewpoints of these two men may have differed, but neither seems to have disputed the other's statements.[45] Dr. Bob very simply stated he believed that A.A.'s basic ideas came from the AAs' study of the Bible. And it seems very clear that this Bible study involved not only the Bible, but also the Bible devotionals, and the Oxford Group and other spiritual literature about the Bible that AAs mentioned and read. Bill Wilson pointed to the Oxford Group in general and to Dr. Sam Shoemaker specifically as the source for A.A.'s ideas. He later described the spiritual principles as "the common property of

---

[45] For a full discussion of A.A.'s six major spiritual sources, see Dick B., *Utilizing A.A.'s Spiritual Roots for Recovery Today* (Kihei, HI: Paradise Research Publications, 1998).

mankind."[46] But Bill was quite specific as to the source of these principles—the Oxford Group and Sam Shoemaker.[47]

We have covered in our other titles the great extent to which the Oxford Group principles and those of Dr. Shoemaker were based on the Good Book. But one cannot read the Oxford Group or Shoemaker writings without encountering the Good Book at every turn. The Oxford Group's founder and leader, Frank Buchman, was described by his biographer as "soaked in the Bible."[48] Buchman's life and teaching, and the lives and teachings of his mentors, were Bible-based and Bible-oriented.

Similarly, Sam Shoemaker's co-worker, Reverend Irving Harris, said Shoemaker was a "Bible Christian." Harris said, "The Scriptures formed the basis of Sam Shoemaker's preaching." He added that Shoemaker's Church provided "a place to learn the how of faith, both in sermons and in groups—How to find God. How to pray. How to read the Bible. How to pass faith on."[49]

Dr. Bob spoke of studying the Bible and Oxford Group philosophy and teachings. Bill Wilson spoke wistfully of these early days of Scripture reading and devotionals.[50] While Bill was specific that A.A. got its principles from the teachings of the

---

[46] See Mel B., *New Wine* (Minnesota: Hazelden Foundation, 1991), p. 3.

[47] See *Alcoholics Anonymous Comes of Age* (New York: Alcoholics Anonymous World Services, Inc., 1957), p. 39; *The Language of the Heart* (New York: The A.A. Grapevine, Inc., 1988), p. 298; *DR. BOB*, pp. 96, 100; *Pass It On*, p. 128; Big Book, p. xvi.

[48] Lean, *On The Tail of a Comet*, p. 157.

[49] W. Irving Harris, *The Breeze of the Spirit* (New York: The Seabury Press, 1978), pp. 18, 25.

[50] *DR. BOB* quotes Bill as follows, "I sort of always felt that something was lost from A.A. when we stopped emphasizing the morning meditation" (p. 178). On page 71, it quotes Bill as follows, "For the next three months, I lived with these two wonderful people [Dr. Bob and Anne Smith] . . . I shall always believe they gave me more than I ever brought them." Each morning, there was a devotion, he recalled. After a long silence, in which they awaited inspiration and guidance, Anne would read from the Bible. "James was our favorite," he said. "Reading from her chair in the corner, she would softly conclude, 'Faith without works is dead.'"

Oxford Group and Shoemaker, the starting point for each co-founder was, whether acknowledged or not, the Good Book.

Dr. Bob was studying the Bible; as were Anne, Henrietta, and the other early AAs—in their Oxford Group "alcoholic squad" meetings.[51] And Dr. Bob and other early Akron AAs referred to themselves as "A Christian Fellowship."[52] Our research on the books in Dr. Bob's library, our interviews of his family and of Henrietta Seiberling's family, and our review of what AAs were studying in Christian literature, other than that of the Oxford Group, make it clear that a record should be made of *all* Dr. Bob's books. They show Dr. Bob's focus on Scripture study, Jesus Christ, the new birth, atonement, prayer, revelation, believing, the Sermon on the Mount, witness, and fellowship, for example.

Dr. Bob's reading involved key Christian sources: (1) The Bible; (2) Christian classics by St. Augustine, Thomas à Kempis, and Brother Lawrence; (3) Studies of the life of Jesus Christ; (4) Daily Bible devotionals such as *The Upper Room*, *My Utmost For His Highest*, and *The Runner's Bible*, as well as those by Mary Tileston, E. Stanley Jones, and Harry Emerson Fosdick; (5) Prayer studies by Oswald Chambers, Glenn Clark, Fosdick, E. Stanley Jones, and others; (6) Well-known books on love by Toyohiko Kagawa and Henry Drummond; (7) New thought books by James Allen, Emmet Fox, and Ralph Waldo Trine; and (8) Many others on all aspects of the Bible and Christian religion.

We conclude this introduction by pointing to a strong comment by Anne Ripley Smith in her Journal. Though she listed, and wrote, in several different portions of her Journal, about a number of important Christian books by Oxford Group writers and others, she added emphatically:

---

[51] See *DR. BOB* for the name "alcoholic squad of the Oxford Group" that they applied to themselves (pp. 137, 117, 100, 128).

[52] *DR. BOB*, p. 118; Bob E. stated this also in his handwritten memo to Lois Wilson on the *Four Absolutes* pamphlet we found at the Archives Exhibit in Akron on Founders Day, 1991. Cf. Thomsen, *Bill W.*, p. 282.

Of course the Bible ought to be the main Source Book of all. No day ought to pass without reading in it.[53]

---

[53] See Dick B., *Anne Smith's Journal* (copy in possession of the author; Pages 16, 48 are numbers of the journal itself and were assigned by A.A. Archives in New York). Compare Lean, *On The Tail of a Comet*, which says Oxford Group Founder, Dr. Frank Buchman's recipe for Bible-reading was, "Read accurately, interpret honestly, apply drastically" (p. 157). Sam Shoemaker's *Realizing Religion* has a chapter entitled, *Driving Power for the New Life* (pp. 58-70). He wrote "we know the Bible is a mine of gold, but we do not know where nor how to begin to dig. . . . The chief thing that I want to emphasize about our use of the Bible is not so much the way each of us shall pursue our study of it, as the setting apart of a definite time each morning for this, together with prayer. . . . Study one book at a time, mastering the thought of it, the plan and dominant ideas. Read what is there, not your own ideas into it (pp. 58, 60, 62). See Samuel M. Shoemaker, Jr., *Realizing Religion* (New York: Association Press, 1921).

2

Sources of Information about His Books

We believe our sources of information as to the books Dr. Bob read are totally reliable. In this chapter, we will review them, one by one, indicating how the sources are identified as we refer to the books in the next chapter and list the sources in the footnotes.

Our first source was Sue Smith Windows, Dr. Bob's daughter. Sue personally showed to the author, at Akron, Ohio, during the 1991 Founders Day Conference there, a substantial number of books that Dr. Bob owned, read, recommended, and loaned out. Many contain Dr. Bob's own signature and home address, with the date he acquired them, and often a notation, "Please return." In December, 1991, Sue mailed the author a lengthy list in her own hand of the remaining books that belonged to and were read by Dr. Bob, and that she said were still in her possession. By her preference, the specific books in her possession are not listed in our book. Instead, those belonging to Sue Smith Windows and those belonging to Dr. Bob's son, Robert R. Smith, are simply labeled in the footnotes, "Owned by family." During the 1992 Founders Day activities, Sue gave us personal access to the books of Dr. Bob she has retained; and we then found still further books he had read and which had not previously been mentioned by Sue or by others. Almost all concerned spiritual subjects.

Our second source was Dr. Bob's son, Robert R. Smith, and Robert's wife, Betty. They inventoried Dr. Bob's books that were still in their possession. In November of 1991, they provided the author with a handwritten list—thirty-five books in all. They confirmed that Dr. Bob had read each. Following the procedure mentioned in the preceding paragraph, we have also labeled these in the footnotes, "Owned by family." Subsequent to a 1991 visit we had with the Smith's, and at our suggestion, Dr. Bob's son presented a large number of Dr. Bob's books to Dr. Bob's Home at 855 Ardmore Avenue in Akron where they could then be seen in a glass case and studied by those interested. Later, the author visited Dr. Bob's son and his wife at their home in Nocona, Texas; and he was permitted to inspect other books still on hand and which were owned, read, recommended, and often loaned out by Dr. Bob.

Third, there were the books listed in Anne Ripley Smith's spiritual Journal. At the request of Sue Smith Windows, A.A. Archives in New York provided the author with a complete xerox copy of Anne Ripley Smith's sixty-four-page Journal. Sue Windows wrote the author that this Journal was compiled by Anne Smith, Dr. Bob's wife, between 1933 and 1939; and the portions that are typed were typed from Anne's notes by her daughter, Sue, sometime in 1937-1938 while Sue was attending business college. On two different pages, Anne Smith listed the books she read and recommended. Anne also devoted several pages to a book by Toyohiko Kagawa, and mentioned an early book by Dr. Sam Shoemaker and a book by E. Stanley Jones.[1] Anne also made reference to Eleanor Napier Forde, an early Oxford Group writer; and Anne's language strongly indicated that Anne had read Miss Forde's foundational book, *The Guidance of God*. In fact, several of Anne's remarks appeared to be quotes from Miss Forde's book. As stated, Dr. Bob's daughter confirmed to the author that Dr.

---

[1] The Kagawa book was *Love: The Law of Life*, discussed later in our book. The Shoemaker book was *One Boy's Influence* (New York: Association Press, 1925). Anne Smith did not specify which of the E. Stanley Jones books she was quoting, and we have not been able to locate the quote.

Bob had read all the books listed in his wife's Journal. These are designated in the footnotes as, *"Anne Smith recommended."*

RHS, the memorial issue of A.A.'s *Grapevine*, which was published at the time of Dr. Bob's death in 1951, listed two books on page 34 that Dr. Bob had sent to another alcoholic. A copy of one is presently in possession of Dr. Bob's family.[2] The other book was mentioned by an early Akron AA in a handwritten memo to Bill Wilson's wife, Lois. That early A.A. member said Dr. Bob recommended the book.[3] We designate these books in the footnotes as, *"RHS mentions."*

Bob E., the early Akron AA we've just mentioned, sent a handwritten memo to Lois Wilson on an Akron A.A. Pamphlet titled, "Four Absolutes." That memo listed three books Dr. Bob regularly provided to alcoholics with whom he worked.[4] These are designated in the footnotes, "Bob E.'s List."

DR. BOB and the Good Oldtimers, A.A.'s official biography of Dr. Bob, specifically mentioned a few of Dr. Bob's books; and we designate these in the footnotes as, *"DR. BOB mentions."*

Clarence S.–who got sober in February, 1938; was one of the original forty pioneer AAs; and was sponsored by Dr. Bob–provided a list of nineteen books he read. These were all recommended to him for study by Dr. Bob.[5]

We have used a final, somewhat speculative source—a list of Oxford Group Literature contained in the Reverend Samuel Shoemaker's Calvary Episcopal Church monthly parish publication—*The Calvary Evangel*. In our first edition, we listed those

---

[2] Nora Smith Holm's *The Runner's Bible*.

[3] The book is James Allen's *As A Man Thinketh*.

[4] The author located, copied, and has in his possession a xerox copy of the handwritten memo by Bob E. of Akron. The copy was obtained courtesy of Gail L., who prepared the Archives Exhibit at the Akron Founders Day Conference in June of 1991. The three books Bob E. mentioned were James Allen's *As A Man Thinketh*, Henry Drummond's *The Greatest Thing in the World*, and Emmet Fox's *The Sermon on the Mount*.

[5] See Dick B., *That Amazing Grace: The Role of Clarence and Grace S. in Alcoholics Anonymous* (San Rafael, CA: Paradise Research Publications, 1996), p. 31.

Oxford Group books recommended by *The Calvary Evangel*—in its March, 1939, issue. During our 1993 visit to the archives of Calvary Episcopal Church in New York, we were allowed to review issues of *The Calvary Evangel* for the entire period of A.A.'s formative years between 1935 and 1939, the period during which AAs were an integral part of the Oxford Group (on the East Coast, until 1937, and in Akron, until 1939). We found and have added to this edition a number of Oxford Group books not mentioned in our prior edition, but which we now know were stocked at the bookroom of Calvary Church, used at Oxford Group meetings, and distributed throughout much of the United States.[6] Still later, the author found at The Episcopal Church Archives in Austin, Texas, an entirely new list of books that Sam Shoemaker himself had inventoried. These are listed in Appendix 2.

Dr. Bob stated several times and in several ways that he had put a good deal of study into the Oxford Group's philosophy and teachings, and had read an immense number of the books they recommended. Yet the number of Oxford Group books owned by his family today, mentioned in other A.A. literature, or specifically recommended by Anne Smith in her Journal, is very limited. Henrietta Seiberling's son, John, wrote the author that Henrietta had read "all the Oxford Group books of the 1930's;" and he and his sister, Dorothy, specifically listed for the author the Oxford Group books they still own or recall their mother's reading.

The Smith family, the Seiberling children, and Henrietta herself—as well as other A.A. sources—all indicate that Henrietta Seiberling had much to do with the spiritual "education" Dr. Bob and Bill received in the summer of 1935 in Akron, and later.

Through the generosity of Mrs. W. Irving Harris, wife of the Rev. W. Irving Harris of the Calvary Episcopal Church staff in New York, the author has in his possession a copy of *The Calvary Evangel* for March, 1939. That *Evangel* contains a list of Oxford

---

[6] See Dick B., *New Light on Alcoholism: The A.A. Legacy from Sam Shoemaker* (Corte Madera, CA, Good Book Publishing Company, 1994), pp. 347-51.

Group Literature stocked and available at the bookroom in the basement of Calvary House in New York in 1939. Calvary House was the virtual headquarters of the Oxford Group in America at that time; and Dr. Frank Buchman—the Oxford Group Founder—lived in Calvary House when he was in New York.[7]

Mrs. W. Irving Harris and her husband lived at Calvary House, during the 1935-1939 period. The Reverend Harris was then a member of the Calvary Church staff. He later became editor of *The Calvary Evangel* (which was subsequently called *Faith At Work)*. And for a time, *The Calvary Evangel* "became very much like a house organ for the Oxford Group, or M.R.A., as this work began to be called."[8] Mrs. Harris wrote the author that she was in charge of the Oxford Group bookstore at Calvary House from 1936 to April of 1938; and that the March, 1939, *Evangel* Oxford Group Literature list "contains all the books we would have carried [at that particular time]."[9]

We discuss the Calvary Church Oxford Group Literature List because we believe either Dr. Bob, Henrietta Seiberling, Anne Smith, or all three, probably read all of these Oxford Group books. Since Henrietta had read "all the Oxford Group books of the 1930's," and since Dr. Bob "had done an immense amount of reading they (the Oxford Group) recommended," we believe Dr. Bob must have read all or most of the Oxford Group literature on

---

[7] Letter to the author, dated October 21, 1991, from Garth Lean, Dr. Frank Buchman's biographer, and an Oxford Group co-worker.

[8] See Irving Harris, *The Breeze of the Spirit* (New York: The Seabury Press, 1978), pp. 70-73.

[9] Statement by Julia C. Harris, dated November 11, 1991, sent to the author, and signed by Mrs. Harris on a xerox copy of *The Calvary Evangel* Oxford Group Literature list for March, 1939. *Evangel* readers were informed that any book on the list would be sent on receipt of check or money order by The Oxford Group, 61 Gramercy Park, New York City. The 1939 list of books will be found at the end of Chapter 3 of our book and has now been supplemented in this edition by adding the books the author recently discovered in previous issues of *The Evangel*. See also the new list from The Episcopal Church Archives, as set forth in Appendix 2.

the *Evangel* list.[10] Calvary Church, which published *The Evangel*, was the primary distributor of Oxford Group literature in America. Thus, even if this list was not the source of the books "recommended" to Dr. Bob by the Oxford Group, it still seems very likely that the books on the list were made available to Dr. Bob, or at least discussed in his presence, by Henrietta Seiberling at the Oxford Group meetings Dr. Bob attended. Henrietta was very much in charge of the Oxford Group meetings in Akron at the home of T. Henry and Clarace Williams. In the next chapter's footnotes, we designate the *Evangel* books as, "Evangel List."

---

[10] In *Co-Founders*, Dr. Bob is quoted as saying he had done "an immense amount of reading they [the Oxford Group] had recommended" (p. 7). Former Congressman John F. Seiberling wrote the author on July 5, 1991, "My mother, I am sure, read all the Oxford Group books of the 1930's." He and his sister, Dorothy Seiberling, listed in writing for the author a number of the Oxford Group books they recalled their mother's having read: *For Sinners Only, Soul Surgery, If I Be Lifted Up, Children of the Second Birth*, and *Inspired Children*. All were Oxford Group books listed in *The Calvary Evangel* issue for March of 1939.

3

The Books Dr. Bob Owned, Read, and Recommended

The Bible

Books about the Bible

1. *God's Great Plan, a Guide to the Bible* by R. Llewelyn Williams.[1]

2. *The Fathers of the Church.*[2]

Christian Classics

1. *The Confessions of St. Augustine.*[3] Dr. Sam Shoemaker, Harry Emerson Fosdick, and a number of Oxford Group writers

---

[1] R. Llewelyn Williams, *God's Great Plan, a Guide to the Bible* (Hoverhill Destiny Publishers, n.d.). Owned by family.

[2] *The Fathers of the Church* (New York: CIMA Publishing, 1947). Owned by family.

[3] *The Confessions of St. Augustine*, trans. by E. B. Pusey (New York: A Cardinal Edition, Pocket Books, 1952). Owned by family; *DR. BOB* mentions, p. 310. See *DR. BOB and the Good Oldtimers* (New York: Alcoholics Anonymous World Services, Inc., 1980).

frequently quoted St. Augustine's *Confessions*—a 1,500 year old Christian classic. The best known quote, perhaps, is "for Thou madest us for Thyself, and our heart is restless, until it repose in Thee" (p. 1). The *Confessions* Introduction contained this exhortation, "Seek for yourself, O man; search for your true self. He who seeks shall find—but, marvel and joy, he will not find himself, he will find God, or, if he find himself, he will find himself in God" (p. x).

2. *The Imitation of Christ* by Thomas à Kempis.[4] The translator said, "As we step back, the picture takes shape: a person stands before God, profoundly alone; God embraces him with a deep and unutterable love; and with great humility he strives to love God in return" (p. xlix). In a chapter entitled, "Counsels on the Spiritual Life," à Kempis said:

> As you meditate on the life of Jesus Christ, you should grieve that you have not tried more earnestly to conform yourself to Him, although you have been a long while in the way of God. A Religious who earnestly and devoutly contemplates the most holy Life and Passion of Our Lord will find it in an abundance of all things profitable and needful to him, nor need he seek any other model than Jesus (pp. 64-65).

3. *The Practice of the Presence of God* by Brother Lawrence.[5] Brother Lawrence said:

> I still believe that all spiritual life consists of practicing God's presence, and that anyone who practices it correctly will soon

---

[4] Thomas à Kempis, *The Imitation of Christ*, A New Reading of the 1441 Latin Autograph Manuscript by William C. Creasy (Georgia: Mercer University Press, 1989). Owned by family.

[5] Brother Lawrence, *The Practice of the Presence of God* (Pennsylvania: Whitaker House, 1982). Betty Smith recalls that Dr. Bob, her father-in-law, read this book. Henrietta Seiberling's family are clear that Henrietta read it. Brother Lawrence was often quoted by Glenn Clark, an author whose books were favorites of Dr. Bob.

attain spiritual fulfillment. To accomplish this, it is necessary for the heart to be emptied of everything that would offend God. He wants to possess your heart completely. Before any work can be done in your soul, God must be totally in control (p. 29).

Brother Lawrence is further quoted:

If someone surrenders himself entirely to God, resolving to do anything for Him, the Lord will protect that person from deception. He will also not allow such a person to suffer through trials for very long, but will give him a way of escape that he might endure it [1 Corinthians 10:13] (p. 15).

The quotes, though written nearly 300 years ago, must sound familiar to AAs. Their Big Book speaks frequently of the power and presence of God (pp. 51, 56, 162). The Brother Lawrence book is filled with insights on how to remain in the presence of God daily.

The Life of Jesus Christ

Dr. Bob's wife, Anne, wrote in her Journal, "One should by all means read at least one book on the life of Christ a year for a while. More would be better."[6] She listed the following books, saying they "are all good." Sue Windows wrote the author that her father read them all; and we included them in our first edition:

1. *Jesus of Nazareth: A Biography* by George A. Barton.[7]

2. *The Life of Jesus Christ* by the Rev. James Stalker.[8]

---

[6] Dick B., *Anne Smith's Journal, 1933-1939* (San Rafael, CA: Paradise Research Publications, 1994), p. 82.

[7] George A. Barton, *Jesus of Nazareth: A Biography* (New York: The Macmillan Company, 1922).

[8] James Stalker, *The Life of Jesus Christ*, new & revised ed. (New York: Fleming H. Revell, 1891).

3. *Studies of the Man Christ Jesus* by Robert E. Speer.[9] Speer formulated the Four Absolutes. He felt these standards—honesty, purity, unselfishness, and love—epitomized the teachings of Jesus. These "Absolutes" substantially influenced Frank Buchman and Sam Shoemaker.[10] They constituted major Oxford Group tenets.[11] They are still used by AAs.[12]

4. *The Jesus of History* by T. R. Glover.[13]

The following are newly-discovered books Dr. Bob owned.[14]

5. *The Manhood of the Master* by Harry Emerson Fosdick.[15]

6. *The Man from Nazareth* by Harry Emerson Fosdick.[16]

7. *Jesus and Our Generation* by Charles Whitney Silkey.[17]

---

[9] Robert E. Speer, *Studies of the Man Christ Jesus* (New York: Fleming H. Revell, 1896).

[10] See Lean, *On the Tail of a Comet*, p. 76, as to Buchman. See Helen Smith Shoemaker, *I Stand By The Door* (New York: Harper & Row, 1967), pp. 24-27, as to Shoemaker.

[11] See Frank N. D. Buchman, *Remaking the World* (London: Blandford Press, 1961), p. 80; A. J. Russell, *For Sinners Only* (London: Hodder & Stoughton, 1932), pp. 319-29; Garth Lean, *On the Tail of a Comet* (Colorado Springs: Helmers & Howard, 1988), pp. 76-77; Dick B., *The Oxford Group & Alcoholics Anonymous*, new, rev. ed. (Kihei, HI: Paradise Research Publications, 1998), pp. 237-46.

[12] Mel B., *New Wine* (Minnesota: Hazelden, 1991), pp. 76, 138.

[13] T. R. Glover, *The Jesus of History* (New York: Association Press, 1930).

[14] Owned by family, or now located at Dr. Bob's Home in Akron.

[15] Harry Emerson Fosdick, *The Manhood of the Master* (London: Student Christian Movement, 1924). Fosdick provided much support to early A.A. *Alcoholics Anonymous Comes of Age* (NY: Alcoholics Anonymous World Services, 1957), pp. 322-24.

[16] Harry Emerson Fosdick, *The Man from Nazareth* (New York: Harper & Brothers, 1949).

[17] Charles Whitney Silkey, *Jesus and Our Generation* (Chicago: University of Chicago Press, 1925).

Daily Bible Devotionals

Much is made today in recovery programs of daily meditation books. The little book, *Twenty-Four Hours a Day*, has sold in the millions and is distributed to patients in many recovery centers, the author having been one of those patients. The book said its readings contain most of the material used in the booklet *For Drunks Only* as well as many passages from the book *God Calling*, edited by the Oxford Group writer, A. J. Russell. Recently, Alcoholics Anonymous itself published a meditation book.[18] The Big Book's Eleventh Step discussion mentions "morning meditations" and "helpful books." And it seems almost certain that the many meditation books, used today in substance abuse recovery programs, had their origins in the daily Bible devotionals used by early AAs.[19] One of these early devotionals—a Methodist quarterly periodical titled *The Upper Room*—was, as we have discussed, said to be "Required Reading" for the people with whom Dr. Bob worked. The following are the devotionals Dr. Bob read and used:

1. *Daily Strength for Daily Needs* by Mary W. Tileston.[20]
Glenn Clark recommended this book "For the Morning Watch."[21] The "Morning Watch" was a term for the Quiet Time set aside each morning by Oxford Group adherents and many other

---

[18] See *Twenty-Four Hours a Day* (Minnesota: Hazelden, 1975); Richmond Walker, *For Drunks Only* (Minnesota: Hazelden, n.d.); The Two Listeners, *God Calling* (Australia: DAYSTAR, 1985); *Daily Reflections* (New York: A.A. World Services, Inc., 1990).

[19] See Dick B., *Good Morning!: Quiet Time, Morning Watch, Meditation, and Early A.A.*, Bridge Builders ed. (Kihei, HI: Paradise Research Publications, 1998).

[20] Mary W. Tileston, *Daily Strength for Daily Needs* (Boston: Roberts Brothers, 1893). Owned by family.

[21] See Glenn Clark, *Fishers of Men* (Boston: Little, Brown, 1928), p. 98.

Christians for private prayer, Bible study, and worship.[22] *The Upper Room* issue, on the page for May 9, 1935, suggested that the "morning watch" may have had its origin in the words of Psalm 5:3.[23] We included a sample page of this devotional in one of our later historical studies.[24]

2. *My Utmost for His Highest* by Oswald Chambers.[25] Sue Windows informed the author that her mother and father frequently used this book as a daily Bible devotional. Lois Wilson said that she and Bill frequently read this devotional.[26] Frank Buchman's biographer wrote us that Chambers' devotional was widely read and recommended within the Oxford Group though Chambers was not an Oxford Group member. Mrs. Irving Harris also confirmed the wide Oxford Group usage of Chambers' book.[27] Each page contained a date; a topic such as "God First;" a Bible verse or verses on the topic; a comment; and Bible citations to study.[28]

---

[22] See Jack C. Winslow, *When I Awake* (London: Hodder & Stoughton, 1938). Winslow was an Oxford Group leader and writer. See also Samuel M. Shoemaker, *Realizing Religion* (New York: Association Press, 1923), p. 61; *The Conversion of the Church* (New York: Fleming H. Revell, 1932), pp. 60-61; Harry Emerson Fosdick, *The Meaning of Prayer* (New York: Association Press, 1926), pp. 75-76; and Charles Hopkins, *John R. Mott, A Biography* (Grand Rapids: John B. Erdmans Publishing, 1979), p. 218. See Dick B., *Good Morning!*, pp. 1-18.

[23] Psalm 5:3 states, "My voice shalt thou hear in the morning, O Lord; in the morning will I direct my prayer unto thee, and will look up." See citation below for *The Upper Room*; and see its discussion of this verse for May 9, 1935, suggesting that this verse may be the origin of the "morning watch."

[24] Dick B., *The Akron Genesis of Alcoholics Anonymous* (Kihei, HI: Paradise Research Publications, 1998), p. 336.

[25] Oswald Chambers, *My Utmost for His Highest* (London: Simpkin Marshall, Ltd. 1927). Owned by family.

[26] See Bill Pittman, *AA The Way It Began* (WA: Glen Abbey Books, 1988), p. 183.

[27] Telephone conversation with the author. This fact was also confirmed by Mark Guldseth, *Streams* (Fritz Creek, Alaska: Fritz Creek Studios, 1982), p. 160.

[28] For a sample, see Dick B., *The Akron Genesis*, p. 334.

3. *The Runner's Bible* by Nora Smith Holm.[29] This interesting book discussed groups of Bible verses under such topics as: "Walk in Love," "Rejoice Always," "In Everything Give Thanks," and "Fear Not, Only Believe." The Bible verses grouped under such titles give exhortation and comfort to the reader on the topics mentioned. The book is not necessarily a "daily" devotional, but is a guide to the study of familiar and "favorite" Bible verses. Dr. Bob did such a study each day as a part of his devotions.[30]

4. *The Upper Room: Daily Devotions for Family and Individual Use.*[31] *DR. BOB and the Good Oldtimers* mentions this periodical frequently; and hence substantiates its wide use in early Akron A.A.[32] Dr. Bob's daughter told us that her mother-in-law, Lucy Galbraith, frequently brought copies to her son, Ernie's, home to be taken to Oxford Group meetings. Sue said Lucy sometimes actually brought the quarterlies to the early A.A. meetings herself.[33] *AA The Way It Began* asserted that the periodical was on Dr. Bob's "Required Reading List" (p. 197). Each devotional page began with a date and then quoted a Bible verse. Next, a comment on the verse. Next, several suggested Bible verses to be read on the topic. Next, a prayer; and finally, the "Thought for the

---

[29] Nora Smith Holm, *The Runner's Bible* (New York: Houghton Mifflin Company, 1915). Owned by family; *RHS* mentions, p. 34.

[30] See *DR. BOB*, p. 314.

[31] This booklet first began publication as a quarterly in April of 1935. It was edited by Grover Carlton Emmons, and was published by the General Committee on Evangelism through the Department of Home Missions, Evangelism, Hospitals, Board of Missions, Methodist Episcopal Church, South, 650 Doctors' Building, Nashville, Tennessee. The author has a copy of the first issue as well as most of the other issues which were published and circulated among early AAs between 1935 and 1939.

[32] See *DR. BOB*, pages 151, 139, 71, 178, 220, 311.

[33] Interview by the author of Sue Smith Windows in Akron, Ohio, during Founders Day Conference in June, 1991.

Day."[34] Many of the topics (though not necessarily the source verse) would be very familiar to AAs today.[35]

5. *Victorious Living* by E. Stanley Jones.[36] The families of Dr. Bob and of Henrietta Seiberling all confirmed that the E. Stanley Jones books were favorites of their parents. And the story of one of the early AAs mentioned *Victorious Living* as well as the Bible as two of the books to which she turned for help.[37]

6. *Abundant Living* by E. Stanley Jones.[38]

7. *Handles of Power* by Lewis L. Dunnington.[39]

8. *I Will Lift Up Mine Eyes* by Glenn Clark.[40]

9. *The Meaning of Prayer* by Harry Emerson Fosdick.[41] In his Preface, Fosdick put his task this way:

---

[34] For a sample page of one of the early issues, see Dick B., *The Akron Genesis*, p. 333.

[35] For example, "My voice shalt thou hear in the morning, O Lord; in the morning I will direct my prayer unto thee: (Psalm 5:3-Eleventh Step); "Be still, and know that I am God" (Psalm 46:1-Third Step); "In all thy ways acknowledge him and he shall direct thy paths" (Proverbs 3:6-Eleventh Step); "Confess your faults one to another" (James 5:16-Fifth Step).

[36] E. Stanley Jones, *Victorious Living* (New York: Abingdon Press, 1936). Owned by family. For a sample page of this daily Bible devotional, see Dick B., *The Akron Genesis*, p. 335.

[37] *Alcoholics Anonymous* (New York: Works Publishing Company, 1939), p. 223.

[38] E. Stanley Jones, *Abundant Living* (New York: Abingdon-Cokesbury Press, 1942). Owned by family; and see John 10:10; Ephesians 3:20.

[39] Lewis L. Dunnington, *Handles of Power* (New York: Abingdon-Cokesbury Press, 1942). Owned by family.

[40] Glenn Clark, *I Will Lift Up Mine Eyes* (New York: Harper & Brothers, 1937). Owned by family.

[41] Harry Emerson Fosdick, *The Meaning of Prayer* (New York: Association Press, 1926). Owned by family. See the section below on "Prayer."

In a study such as this, the Bible is the invaluable laboratory manual which records all phases of man's life with God and God's dealing with man. . . . Each chapter is divided into three sections: Daily Readings, Comment for the Week, and Suggestions for Thought and Discussion. This arrangement for daily devotional reading—"The Morning Watch," for intensive study, and for study group discussion—has met such wide acceptance in my previous book that it has been continued here.[42]

For each day, Fosdick presented a thought, Bible verses for study, and a commentary. He then concluded with a prayer for that day.

Prayer

Probably there is no single category of books that Dr. Bob owned and read that evidences more extensive study than the books he read on prayer. A.A.'s co-founder, Bill Wilson, was particularly respectful of Dr. Bob's primacy in that area. Bill said:

He [Dr. Bob] prayed, not only for his own understanding, but for different groups of people who requested him to pray for them. . . . I was always glad to think that I was included in these prayers. . . . And I sort of depended on him to get me into heaven. Bob was far ahead of me in that sort of activity (*DR. BOB*, p. 315).

We will list here the authors and books Dr. Bob read on the subject of prayer and, where the author was one favored by Dr. Bob, leave discussion of details to that part of our book on "Authors of Special Interest to Dr. Bob."

1. **Glenn Clark**. Clark's books were powerhouses on prayer. His first, *The Soul's Sincere Desire*, was immensely popular in the

---

[42] Fosdick, *The Meaning of Prayer*, p. xi.

1930's; and Dr. Bob and other early Akron AAs used it widely.[43] Other Clark books on prayer were *The Lord's Prayer and Other Talks on Prayer from The Camps Farthest Out, I Will Lift Up Mine Eyes*, and *How to Find Health through Prayer*.[44]

2. **Starr Daily**. Daily's book, *Recovery*, records many extraordinary healings effected through the personal ministry of Rev. Roland J. Brown, who was a pastor of the Parkside Baptist Church in Chicago at the time of Daily's writing. Daily called his book "a book of miracles, a document of answered prayers."[45]

3. **Lewis L. Dunnington**. Dunnington was pastor of Endion Methodist Church in Duluth, Minnesota. In *Handles of Power*, he proposed, "a definite and simple technique of prayer for unlocking the illimitable resources of God's abundance."[46] He focused on "Silent Communion Cards," which he advocated repeating slowly at the beginning and end of each day, and as often through the day as possible. An example is a card based on the phrase, "God the Father dwells within me and fulfills every need" (p. 73).

4. **Mary Baker Eddy**. Mrs. Eddy's *Christian Science Textbook with Key to the Scriptures* was the basic textbook used by Christian

---

[43] Glenn Clark, *The Soul's Sincere Desire* (Boston: Little, Brown, and Company, 1925). Sue Smith Windows informed the author in a personal interview at Akron in June, 1991, that the Clark books were favorites of Dr. Bob. Henrietta Seiberling's children particularly mentioned this Clark book as part of Henrietta's reading. Nell Wing, Bill Wilson's secretary, lists the book as among those early AAs read. See Pittman, *AA The Way It Began*, p. 192. Owned by family.

[44] Glenn Clark, *The Lord's Prayer and Other Talks on Prayer from The Camps Farthest Out* (MN: Macalester Park Publishing Co., 1932); *I Will Lift Up Mine Eyes*, supra; and *How to Find Health through Prayer* (Harper & Brothers, 1940). All owned by family.

[45] Starr Daily, *Recovery* (St. Paul, Minnesota: Macalester Park Publishing Company, 1948), p. 11. Owned by family.

[46] See Dunnington, *Handles of Power,* p. 10. Owned by family.

Scientists.[47] It set forth the Christian Science method for using the Christian Science textbook and the Bible for deliverance. Both Bill Wilson and Dr. Bob studied this work.[48]

5. **Charles and Cora Filmore**. Their book, *Teach Us to Pray*, focused on the Unity approach.[49]

6. **Harry Emerson Fosdick**. Fosdick was very supportive of early A.A.; and Dr. Bob owned and read a large number of his books.[50] Fosdick's *The Meaning of Prayer* was recommended by Anne Smith in her Journal.[51] Fosdick frequently quoted Thomas à Kempis. Fosdick's little book is a compendium on Christian prayer and contains a number of expressions familiar to AAs. For example, Fosdick said:

> Prayer opens our lives to God so that his will can be done in and through us, because in true prayer we habitually put ourselves into the attitude of *willingness to do whatever God wills* (p. 59).

> Prayer . . . when it is at its best, never says, Thy will be *changed*, but it says tremendously, Thy will be *done*! (p. 66).[52]

7. **Emmet Fox**. We will discuss Fox's books in our sections on "The Sermon on the Mount" and "Authors of Special Interest to

---

[47] Mary Baker Eddy, *Science and Health with Key to the Scriptures* (Boston: Published by the Trustees under the Will of Mary Baker G. Eddy, 1916). Owned by family.

[48] See *Lois Remembers* (New York: Al-Anon Family Group Headquarters, 1979), p. 84; Ernest Kurtz, *Not-God* (MN, Hazelden, 1991), p. 54; and Pittman, *AA The Way It Began*, p. 150.

[49] Charles and Cora Filmore, *Teach Us to Pray* (Lee's Summit, Missouri: Unity School of Christianity, 1950). *DR. BOB* mentions, p. 310.

[50] Mel B., *New Wine*, pp. 145-47.

[51] See Fosdick, *The Meaning of Prayer*; and Dick B., *Anne Smith's Journal, 1933-1939*, p. 14.

[52] Compare Big Book, pp. 85, 88.

Dr. Bob." But most of Fox's works do belong, as well, in this section on Prayer. Dr. Bob owned a Fox pamphlet entitled, *Getting Results By Prayer*.[53] And Fox's *The Sermon on the Mount* contained a comprehensive study of both the Sermon on the Mount and the Lord's Prayer.[54] In *The Sermon on the Mount*, Fox called the Lord's Prayer the "greatest of all prayers" (p. 162). He said it contained "the implied command that we are to pray not only for ourselves but for all mankind" (p. 166). He added:

> Our business is to bring our whole nature as fast as we can into conformity with the Will of God, by constant prayer and unceasing, though unanxious watching. "Our wills are ours to make them Thine" (p. 174).

Fox then quoted the saying of St. Augustine we previously mentioned, "Thou hast made us for Thyself, and our hearts are restless until they repose in Thee" (*The Sermon on the Mount*, p. 175).

8. **Gerald Heard**. Dr. Bob owned and read Heard's *A Preface to Prayer*.[55] A number of Heard's books were recommended by Glenn Clark as "stimulating to prayer and thought."[56] The author has also learned that Heard was a friend of Bill Wilson's.[57]

9. **E. Stanley Jones**. Dr. Bob owned and read a large number of Jones's books. We will discuss them further in our section on "The Sermon on the Mount" and elsewhere. Glenn Clark often

---

[53] Owned by family.

[54] Emmet Fox, *The Sermon on the Mount* (New York: Harper & Row, 1934).

[55] Gerald Heard, *A Preface to Prayer* (New York: Harper & Brothers, 1944). Owned by family.

[56] Glenn Clark, *Two or Three Gathered Together* (New York: Harper & Brothers. 1942), pp. 74-75.

[57] *Pass It On* (New York: Alcoholics Anonymous World Services, 1984), pp. 290, 368, 370-71, 375.

recommended Jones's books in connection with prayer.[58] See Glenn Clark's interesting discussion of his work with E. Stanley Jones, Toyohiko Kagawa, and others in the prayer realm during World War II.[59] Jones's *Victorious Living*, contained Bible verses for each day of the year under such titles as "How Can I Find God," "What Is Conversion," and "The Power That Gives Release."[60] This book contained much on prayer. Since Anne Smith recommended "all" the Jones books of the time; and Dr. Bob read all those books, we believe this was a book he read.[61]

10. **Frank Laubach**. Dr. Bob owned and read Laubach's *Prayer (Mightiest Force in the World)*.[62] Laubach was one of those who worked with Glenn Clark at The Camps Farthest Out, the retreat attended by Dr. Bob and his wife.[63]

11. **Charles M. Layman**, *A Primer of Prayer*.[64]

12. **Rufus Mosely**, *Perfect Everything*.[65]

13. **William R. Parker**. Parker's *Prayer Can Change Your Life* is mentioned in *DR. BOB* (p. 310). Parker said he had a Key, the discovery of "the Kingdom of Heaven exactly where Jesus of

---

[58] Clark, *Two or Three Gathered Together*, p. 74; *Fishers of Men*, p. 97.

[59] Glenn Clark, *A Man's Reach* (New York: Harper & Brothers, 1949), pp. 269-79.

[60] E. Stanley Jones, *Victorious Living* (New York: The Abingdon Press, 1936), pp. 30, 52, 273.

[61] Glenn Clark recommended this book. See *Two or Three Gathered Together*, p. 74.

[62] Frank C. Laubach, *Prayer (Mightiest Force in the World)* (New York: Fleming H. Revell, 1946). Owned by family.

[63] Betty Smith, Dr. Bob's daughter-in-law, informed the author in a telephone interview in December, 1991, that the Smiths attended The Camps Farthest Out and "loved it." For a discussion of Clark's camps, see Clark, *A Man's Reach*, pp. 250-51.

[64] Charles M. Layman, *A Primer of Prayer* (Nashville, Tidings, 1949). Owned by family.

[65] Rufus Mosely, *Perfect Everything* (MN: Macalester Park Publishing, 1949). Owned by family.

Nazareth had said it was, and is, within" (p. x). He said the purpose of his book was "to reveal the Key, detail our experiments, and show precisely how prayer was applied to individual problems by following the directions of the successful prayers of the past" (p. xi).[66]

14. **F. L. Rawson**, *The Nature of True Prayer*.[67] This book was first printed in 1918. It covers such subjects as: (a) the need to understand the nature of God; (b) a concept of God in heaven; (c) the importance of thinking only of God and praying without ceasing; (d) the importance of daily prayer; (e) how to pray; (f) selflessness and purity; (g) forgiveness of sins; (h) spiritual realities; (i) helping beginners; (j) the evolution of divine healing; (k) grace and the second coming of Christ; (l) Jesus the Christ; and (m) the healing of sin.

The Sermon on the Mount

We emphasize again that the primary focus of both Dr. Bob and his wife, Anne, was on the Bible itself—not on books about subjects *in* the Bible.[68] Dr. Bob cited the Sermon on the Mount (Matthew chapters 5-7) as containing the underlying philosophy of A.A.[69] A good deal has been said in A.A. about Emmet Fox and his book on the Sermon, but Dr. Bob's reading on the Sermon was

---

[66] Dr. William R. Parker and Elaine St. Johns, *Prayer Can Change Your Life: A New Edition of a Modern Classic* (New York: Prentice Hall Press, 1957).

[67] F. L. Rawson, *The Nature of True Prayer*, 7th ed. (Woking, Surrey, UK: The Society for Spreading the Knowledge of True Prayer, 1977). Owned by family.

[68] See *DR. BOB* at page 96, where Dr. Bob mentions the specific portions of the Bible itself that were "absolutely essential," namely, the Sermon on the Mount, the 13th Chapter of 1 Corinthians, and the Book of James. See also our quote above from Anne Smith's Journal, at page 16. And see Pittman, *AA The Way It Began*, at page 197, where the specific portions of the King James Version are set forth at the *top* of what that author called "Dr. Bob's Required Reading List."

[69] *DR. BOB*, p. 228.

not confined to Fox's book. The following are the books Dr. Bob studied on the specific topic of Jesus Christ's sermon:

1. *Studies in the Sermon on the Mount* by Oswald Chambers.[70] Chambers had a highly significant approach to the Sermon on the Mount. He said that Jesus's message can only produce despair unless one has received the Holy Spirit. Chambers did a line-by-line study of the Sermon, but commenced with this admonition:

> Beware of placing our Lord as Teacher first instead of as Saviour. That tendency is prevalent today, and it is a dangerous tendency. We must know Him first as Saviour before His teaching has any meaning for us, or before it has any meaning other than an ideal which leads us to despair. . . . If Jesus is only a Teacher, then all He can do is to tantalize us by erecting a standard we cannot come anywhere near. But if we know Him first as Saviour, by being born again from above, we know that He did not come to teach us only: *He came to make us what He teaches we should be.* The Sermon on the Mount is a statement of the life we will live when the Holy Spirit is having His way with us (p. i).

2. *The Christ of the Mount* by E. Stanley Jones.[71] Jones told of a group with which he met in a Himalayan retreat who "asked ourselves whether in Christ we had a message that was vital and inescapable if we were to find life and God." Jones said, "We were driven at once to the Sermon on the Mount" (p. 7). Jones contended the Sermon on the Mount is not in Christian Creeds, but should be. He suggested a creed that says, "I believe in the Sermon on the Mount and in its way of life, and I intend, God helping me, to embody it" (p. 12). He believed the history of Christendom would have been different had there been such a creed. He said, "The greatest need of modern Christianity is the

---

[70] Oswald Chambers, *Studies in the Sermon on the Mount* (London: Simpkin, Marshall, Ltd., n.d.). Owned by family.

[71] E. Stanley Jones, *The Christ of the Mount: A Working Philosophy of Life* (New York: The Abingdon Press, 1931). Owned by family.

rediscovery of the Sermon on the Mount as the only practical way to live" (p. 14). Speaking of the receipt of the Holy Spirit on Pentecost [in Acts 2], he added:

> Pentecost had the content of the Sermon on the Mount in it and therefore the power manifested was Christian. Pentecost divorced from the Sermon on the Mount is spiritual pow-wow instead of spiritual power (p. 18).

3. *The Sermon on the Mount* by Emmet Fox. Fox did a detailed study in this book of both the Sermon on the Mount and the Lord's Prayer. His book has been much mentioned in A.A., and we shall have more to say of it in the section discussing favored authors.[72] Dr. Bob often read and recommended this Emmet Fox book.

4. *The Soul's Sincere Desire, The Lord's Prayer and Other Talks on Prayer from The Camps Farthest Out,* and *I Will Lift Up Mine Eyes* by Glenn Clark. Each of the foregoing books included a study on prayer, with great emphasis on the Lord's Prayer which, of course, is part of the Sermon on the Mount (see Matthew 6:9-13). If Dr. Bob had a "Required Reading List," the Lord's Prayer was given a special place in that list, according to the list's originator. The resilience of the Lord's Prayer in the A.A. of today is evident from the fact that it is the prayer used at the conclusion of almost every A.A. meeting.[73]

---

[72] *DR. BOB* mentions, p. 310. Bob E.'s List. *AA The Way It Began* includes it in the ten books Nell Wing, Bill Wilson's secretary, said early AAs read; and see lengthy discussion in Mel B., *New Wine*, pp. 105-06, 111-14.

[73] The author personally attended A.A. meetings in Marin County, California, almost daily for five years. Almost every meeting ended with the Lord's Prayer. He found this to be true at A.A. meetings he has attended in the San Francisco Bay Area, and at A.A. Conferences and meetings throughout Northern California, and in Arkansas, Hawaii, Kentucky, Maryland, Minnesota, New York, Washington, West Virginia, and Ohio. But see Mel B.'s suggestion in *New Wine* that the days of the Lord's Prayer in A.A. meetings may be numbered. Mel opines, "The purpose of A.A. is to help alcoholics, not simply to promote use of a certain prayer" (Mel B., *New Wine*, p. 157). This opinion, possibly

(continued...)

Love

Dr. Bob simmered A.A.'s Twelve Steps to two principles—love and service.[74] And he certainly read some powerful Christian works on love. They were:

1. *Love: The Law of Life* by Toyohiko Kagawa.[75] Anne Smith devoted four of the sixty-four pages of her Journal to Kagawa's *Love*. Dr. Bob read and studied *Love*; and Glenn Clark spoke frequently of Kagawa in Clark's autobiography.[76] Kagawa was a Christian pastor in Japan. He is said to have lived out utterly the life of love, which he conceived to have been the essence of Christ's teaching. He wrote at least five books on the Christian religion, constituting his interpretation, from different aspects, of the significance of Jesus. He was involved in the labor and peasant movement in Japan and was involved in statistics and politics. In the first chapter of *Love*, Kagawa wrote, "Where Love is, there is God. Love is my all in all" (p. 47). Kagawa wrote on every aspect of Love: Love and Creation, Physical and Psychic Love, Love and Sexual Desire, Love and Romance, Love and Marriage, the Ethics of Love, Love and Law, Love and Violence, Love and Economics, Love and Society, and many others—the last being Love and God.

---

[73] (...continued)
growing in strength, should be contrasted with the fact that early AAs in Akron considered themselves a "Christian Fellowship" and were endeavoring with great success to follow the precepts of Jesus Christ, among which was his direction to Judeans to pray the Lord's Prayer. See, for example, *DR. BOB*, pp. 118: "Dr. Bob was a prominent man in Akron. Everybody knew him. When he stopped drinking, people asked, 'What's this not-drinking-liquor club you've got over there?' 'A Christian fellowship,' he'd reply." See also *DR. BOB* and its discussion of the Frank Amos report, pp. 128-32, 134-36.

[74] *DR. BOB*, p. 338.

[75] Toyohiko Kagawa, *Love: The Law of Life* (Philadelphia: The John C. Winston Company, 1929). Owned by family. Anne Smith recommended.

[76] Clark, *A Man's Reach*, pp. 256, 258, 261-64, 276, 278.

2. *The Greatest Thing in the World* by Henry Drummond.[77] This tiny booklet contained Henry Drummond's study of 1 Corinthians 13. The Corinthians chapter *and* Drummond's book were on Dr. Bob's "Required Reading List."[78] The famous thirteenth chapter of 1 Corinthians has been called the "love chapter." In his study, Drummond specified nine ingredients of love that he found in the Corinthians chapter: patience, kindness, humility, generosity, courtesy, unselfishness, good temper, guilelessness, and sincerity. Many of these ingredients can be found in A.A.'s design for living in the Big Book. In *DR. BOB*, Dorothy S. M. recounts:

> Once when I was working on a woman in Cleveland, I called and asked him [Dr. Bob], "What do I do for somebody who is going into D.T.'s?" He told me to give her the medication, and he said, "When she comes out of it and she decides she wants to be a different woman, get her Drummond's *The Greatest Thing in the World*. Tell her to read it through every day for 30 days, and she'll be a different woman" (p. 310).

Bob E., an early AA in Akron, wrote Bill W.'s wife, Lois, that Dr. Bob frequently gave this booklet out to the people with whom he worked.[79]

3. *The Soul's Sincere Desire* by Glenn Clark.[80] Clark had the following to say on love and prayer:

> Now we come to the most essential of all the laws of Prayer: there must be Love in it (Clark then quotes 1 Corinthians 13). And he [Paul] might have added: And though there be prayers,

---

[77] Henry Drummond, *The Greatest Thing in the World* (New Jersey: Spire Books, Fleming H. Revell, 1968). This essay was written about 1884 and has been published over and over. Owned by family. Bob E.'s List. *DR. BOB* mentions, pp. 151, 310-11.

[78] Pittman, *AA: The Way It Began*, p. 197.

[79] See previous reference to Bob E.'s Memo to Lois Wilson.

[80] Owned by family.

they shall fail; but if love be in the prayer it shall not fail. Jesus wrought not a single miracle where He did not first love, and where the love was not returned unto Him. The greater the miracle the greater the love (pp. 69-70).

When congregations come together to pray, not merely to listen to a sermon or to go through a ritual, when love lives in the prayers and self is forgotten, then we may expect miracles again: for the blind to see, the lame to walk, and those possessed of fear and terror to be set free from demons (p. 73).

The Oxford Group

Dr. Bob had been with the Oxford Group for two-and-a-half years before he met Bill Wilson. And Dr. Bob himself pointed out the Oxford Group focus on service. Oxford Group meetings emphasized Sharing by Witness and helping others to a Life Change, as Oxford Group people called it. Thus Dr. Bob commented on what he received from Bill Wilson via the Oxford Group as follows: "Bill had acquired their idea of service. I had not."[81] Dr. Bob later emphasized that the Twelve Steps themselves simply amounted to love and service. He had read lots about love in the Bible and in the writings of Clark, Drummond, Kagawa, and others. And there was plenty in the Oxford Group writings on service. We have thus far located only eight Oxford Group books in possession of Dr. Bob's family—other than books by Dr. Sam Shoemaker, an East Coast leader in the Group. But these eight books did thoroughly cover Oxford Group principles and practices. And all were on *The Calvary Evangel's* Oxford Group book lists. They are:

---

[81] *DR. BOB*, p. 72.

1. *For Sinners Only* by A. J. Russell.[82] Russell was a British writer and journalist. His book told a good many stories about Oxford Group people including founder, Dr. Frank Buchman, and one of their American leaders, Dr. Samuel Shoemaker. Russell covered the nuts and bolts of Oxford Group principles and practices, with chapters on "Sin," "Restitution," and other Oxford Group concepts. He outlined Oxford Group ideas about God's having a plan and mankind's need to fit in with it; about God's guidance and God's power being available for all those who chose to work with the plan. Russell covered Sharing by Confession and by Witness, early morning listening to God in Quiet Time, Fellowship, Surrender, Life-Changing, the Four Absolutes, and the "miracle" at Reverend Sam Shoemaker's Calvary Church.

2. *He That Cometh* by Geoffrey Allen.[83] Allen laid out some important Oxford Group ideas about coming from lonely individualism "into a deep fellowship of common need and common obedience with other disciples of the Christ" (Preface). He pointed out that people must start their journey to God by coming as babes. He discussed being born again, sin, service, listening to God, and love.

3. *Soul Surgery* by Howard A. Walter.[84] This book on personal evangelism described in detail an "art" Dr. Frank Buchman developed for bringing people to Christ and changing their lives. Its five, major life-changing concepts seem readily

---

[82] A. J. Russell, *For Sinners Only* (London: Hodder & Stoughton, 1932). Owned by family. Anne Smith mentions. *DR. BOB* mentions, p. 310. Nell Wing said it was read by early AAs. And the book was on Dr. Bob's "Required Reading List" (See Pittman, *AA The Way It Began*, pp. 192, 197).

[83] Geoffrey Allen, *He That Cometh* (New York: The Macmillan Company, 1933). Anne Smith mentions.

[84] Howard A. Walter, *Soul Surgery: Some Thoughts on Incisive Personal Work* (Calcutta: Association Press, 1919). Owned by family. *DR. BOB* mentioned its concepts: soul surgery, and the five C's—Confidence, Conviction, Confession, Conversion, and Conservation (p. 54).

identifiable in A.A. today. (1) *Confidence* comprehended not only A.A.'s technique of sharing by confession, but also its program of working with another through gaining that person's confidence. (2) *Confession* found its way directly to A.A.'s Fifth Step. (3) *Conviction* described an individual's need for a deep conviction of sin—that the person must recognize his own need to change, something covered by A.A.'s Sixth Step. (4) *Conversion* described the Surrender process incorporated into A.A.'s Third and Seventh Steps. (5) *Conservation* (or "Continuation," as it was also called) corresponded to A.A.'s Tenth, Eleventh, and Twelfth Steps, which involve "maintaining" one's life-change and communicating to others the means by which one's life change was accomplished.

4. *What is The Oxford Group?* by the Layman with a Notebook.[85] Dr. Bob owned and loaned several copies of this book. It was a primer for the Oxford Group. It explained the Oxford Group. It covered the Four Absolutes—Honesty, Purity, Unselfishness, and Love—which it said were the keys to the kind of spiritual life God wishes us to lead. It detailed four spiritual activities which the Oxford Group advocated "to be spiritually reborn, and to live in the state in which these four points [the Four Absolutes] are the guides to our life in God" (p. 8). It described the four spiritual activities as: (1) Sharing of our sins and temptations with another Christian whose life was given to God, and using Sharing as Witness to help others, still unchanged, to recognize and acknowledge their sins. (2) Surrender of the life into God's keeping and direction. (3) Restitution. (4) Listening to, accepting, relying on God's Guidance, "and carrying it out in everything we do or say, great or small" (pp. 8-9). A student of A.A. can readily find the following A.A. Step concepts in the foregoing four "activities": (1) Acknowledgement of shortcomings and confession (Steps Four and Five), (2) Working with others (Step Twelve), (3) Becoming willing to change and asking God for

---

[85] The Layman with a Notebook, *What Is The Oxford Group?* (London: Oxford University Press, 1933). Owned by family.

help in that process (Steps Six and Seven), (4) Making the decision to change (Steps Three and Seven), (5) Making amends (Steps Eight and Nine), (6) Relying on prayer and meditation for God's guidance and power (Step Eleven), and (7) Practicing spiritual principles in all one's affairs (Step Twelve).

5. *Life Changers* by Harold Begbie.[86] This was one of the earliest books written about Oxford Group Founder, Dr. Frank N. D. Buchman, and his life-changing program. It was widely read in the Oxford Group, in Shoemaker's church circle, and in early A.A.

6. *Twice-Born Men* by Harold Begbie.[87] Though this book was written by Begbie long before there was an Oxford Group, the book itself was very popular in the Oxford Group. And it set the stage for the many narrative stories in the Oxford Group about conversions, the new birth, and life change. The story telling was often called "sharing." The theme was adopted by Sam Shoemaker when he wrote his titles, *Twice-Born Ministers* and *Children of the Second Birth*. Anne Smith highly recommended the reading of these life-changing narratives. The practice of sharing life-changing experiences at meetings became the heart of story telling in today's A.A. meetings and literature.

7. *New Lives for Old* by Amelia S. Reynolds.[88] This account of life changes through Oxford Group practices was popular in Shoemaker's Calvary Church. The author found a copy in the archives at Calvary Church in New York during his 1993 visit there.

---

[86] Harold Begbie, *Life Changers: Narratives of a Recent Movement in the Spirit of Personal Religion* (London: Mills & Boon, Ltd., 1932). Owned by family.

[87] Harold Begbie, *Twice-Born Men* (New York: Fleming H. Revell, 1909). Owned by family.

[88] Amelia S. Reynolds, *New Lives for Old* (New York: Fleming H. Revell, 1929). Anne Smith recommended.

8. *One Thing I Know* by A. J. Russell.[89] After he had written the immensely popular Oxford Group book, *For Sinners Only*, Russell apparently found himself under fire for not having said enough about the Christian concepts of Atonement, the Virgin Birth, the Star of Bethlehem, and the "Sacraments of the Gospels." Russell said he wrote this second book to state, in language clear, simple, and emphatic, an unqualified belief in the divinity of Jesus Christ and his atonement on Calvary—and also to underline his sincere desire for Christian unity.[90]

Dr. Samuel M. Shoemaker

Bill Wilson attributed the Twelve Steps in large part to Dr. Samuel M. Shoemaker; yet the author found no evidence of any books by Shoemaker in Bill's possession at his home at Stepping Stones in Bedford Hills or elsewhere, other than a book written after 1939.[91] Dr. Bob's family owns virtually no Shoemaker books. However, Anne Smith did recommend the following in her Journal, and all are on *The Calvary Evangel's* Oxford Group book list. Sue Smith Windows confirmed to the author in writing that her father, Dr. Bob, read the books. They are:

1. *Children of the Second Birth.*[92] Shoemaker narrated the stories of a number of people in New York who were born again

---

[89] A. J. Russell, *One Thing I Know* (New York: Harper & Brothers, 1933). Owned by family.

[90] For an extended discussion, see Dick B., *The Oxford Group & Alcoholics Anonymous*, pp. 212-13. One A.A. oldtimer informed the author that he [the A.A. oldtimer] had in his possession a copy of *One Thing I Know*, which contained an inscription by Dr. Bob's wife, Anne Smith.

[91] For a thorough study of the Shoemaker influence on A.A. ideas and of Bill Wilson's relationship with Shoemaker, see Dick B., *New Light on Alcoholism: The A.A. Legacy from Sam Shoemaker* (Corte Madera, CA: Good Book Publishing Company, 1994).

[92] Samuel M. Shoemaker, *Children of the Second Birth* (New York: Fleming H. Revell, 1927).

through a Calvary Church conversion experience that initiated a new life for them. He pointed out that, although the conversion is the starting point, all subsequent life is a development of a relationship with God. He said the daily focal point of a reborn life is the Quiet Time, where "we pray and read the Bible. But the distinguishing element of a Quiet Time is listening for the guidance of God" (p. 16). Shoemaker's last words in this book were, "It will be a great day for the Christian cause when the world begins to realize that 'Thy will be done' does not belong on tombstones, but ought to be graven into the lives of eager men and women who have enlisted in God's warfare beyond return and beyond recall" (p. 187).

2. *Confident Faith*.[93] This was a collection of Shoemaker sermons on believing. Shoemaker stated "the supreme confidence is faith in Almighty God" (p. 17). He said the secret of faith and the secret of confidence were: "Just keep looking at Jesus Christ with your will set His way. That will be enough" (p. 20). He explained what Christ meant to him: (1) An historical character, a mortal man. (2) The revelation, in time and finite life, of the character of Infinite God. (3) The Supreme Interpreter of Life, and. (4) Rescuer from sin (pp. 35-47). Shoemaker spoke of the Communion of the Saints "who love and serve" the Lord (p. 93). And he dealt with Saul's conversion which, he believed, simply found Saul in "willing surrender of the self to God and His mercy and His plan, as represented in the words, 'What shall I do, Lord?'" (pp. 114-15). Shoemaker concluded with "the romance of real religion," as he called it: (1) The colossal romance in cooperating with the Spirit that controls this universe. (2) The romance of a relationship between God and those who honestly love and seek His will. (3) The romance of a relationship which comes to pass between those who find themselves thus cooperating with God. (4) The romance of a fight to free the souls of men

---

[93] Samuel M. Shoemaker, *Confident Faith* (New York: Fleming H. Revell, 1932). Owned by family.

from ignorance, selfishness, and sin. (5) The romance of a risk to bet everything you have on God.

3. *If I Be Lifted Up*.[94] This was Shoemaker's book about the Cross. The book's theme was from the words of Jesus in John 12:32, "And I, if I be lifted up from the earth, will draw all *men* unto me." Shoemaker said that, in these words, Jesus "sees the Prince of this world—the spirit of worldliness, I suppose we should say—expelled" (p. 11). Shoemaker believed the Cross would draw suffering people because "misery loves company." It would draw sinning people because they can see "His disapproval of sin, and His suffering for our sin." It would draw thinking people because "suffering love, bearing the burdens of others, remains life's last word" (pp. 12-15). In words familiar to AAs, Shoemaker said:

> [The Cross] restores us as the conscious children of God's love. Its final word is not concerned with how little we *can do* for ourselves, but with how much God *has done* for us (p. 115).[95]

He concluded:

> Let us never forget to tell men that their redemption stands in the Cross of Christ: but let us never forget to tell them also that the appropriation of redemption stands in their own choice and design (p. 172).

---

[94] Samuel M. Shoemaker, *If I Be Lifted Up* (New York: Fleming H. Revell, 1931).

[95] Compare the following remark in A.A.'s "Big Book," where Bill Wilson said of his friend, Ebby Thacher, who carried the Oxford Group message to Bill: "But my friend [Ebby] sat before me, and he made the point blank declaration that God had done for him what he could not do for himself. His human will had failed" (p. 11). Bill then incorporated the same thought in the Big Book's "promises" when he wrote at page 84, "We will suddenly realize that God is doing for us what we could not do for ourselves."

4. *The Conversion of the Church.*[96] Shoemaker said he believed the primary work of the Church was the re-making of the inner lives of individuals, through the power of the living Christ (p. 11). He then discussed the sins "that hold us back from the fullness of spiritual power" (p. 30). He listed pride, exclusiveness, silence or hypocrisy in affectional life, "resting his case in a point of view," and fear. He then described the Oxford Group life-changing process of confession, surrender, and continuance. Then living in touch with God through Scripture reading, prayer, guidance, and fellowship.

5. *Twice-Born Ministers.*[97] In this book, a dozen men in the ministry told of their experience of conversion, or rebirth. Shoemaker said that, for a Christian, conversion ultimately means a complete experience of Jesus Christ. The ministers spoke of honesty with self, seeking the kingdom of God first, surrender, confession, the break with particular sins, restitution and forgiveness, Quiet Time, and the peace that comes from life-change.

6. *One Boy's Influence.*[98] Anne Smith discussed this little booklet at some length in her Journal. Shoemaker told the story of how he led a young man to a conversion experience and then impressed upon the young man the vital importance of passing on to others the message about the experience. Shoemaker was teaching, "You have to give it away to keep it."

7. *Pamphlets.* Two Shoemaker pamphlets are still in possession of Dr. Bob's family. We also found them with the copy of Anne's

---

[96] Samuel M. Shoemaker, *The Conversion of the Church* (New York: Fleming H. Revell, 1932).

[97] Samuel M. Shoemaker, *Twice-Born Ministers* (New York: Fleming H. Revell, 1929).

[98] Samuel Moor Shoemaker, Jr., *One Boy's Influence* (New York: Association Press, 1925).

Journal located at Stepping Stones. The first was titled, *Three Levels of Life*. It was published in the 13th chapter of *Confident Faith*.[99] Shoemaker's three levels were: (1) Instinctive desire; (2) Conscientiousness; and (3) Grace. And he said:

> God help us all to be buoyed above our carelessness, above our carefulness, into the region of His care for us, into the free upper ether of His grace! (*Confident Faith*, p. 166).

The second pamphlet was titled, *What If I Had But One Sermon to Preach?*, and was published in the first chapter of Shoemaker's *Religion That Works*.[100] The topic was John 17:3:

> And this is life eternal, that they might know thee the only true God, and Jesus Christ, whom thou hast sent.

Shoemaker said, if he had but one sermon to preach, its subject would be the homesickness of the human soul for God. He said we all thwart the spiritual nature by sin. The Cross is the medicine of the world. Human beings can be lifted up by conversion. Man must be born again by utter self-dedication to the will of God; and the way is acceptance of God in Christ Jesus.[101]

---

[99] *Confident Faith* is owned by Dr. Bob's family.

[100] Samuel M. Shoemaker, *Religion That Works* (New York: Fleming H. Revell, 1928). This pamphlet is owned by Dr. Bob's family and was included in the copy of Anne Smith's Journal that the author was able to inspect at Bill's home at Stepping Stones.

[101] For a list of a good many other Shoemaker books which were available for reading in the 1930's, most of which were probably read by Dr. Bob, see Dick B., *New Light on Alcoholism: The A.A. Legacy from Sam Shoemaker*, pp. 319, 347-51, 353-55. And see our discussion below of the Oxford Group Literature List in Shoemaker's parish publication, *The Calvary Evangel*.

Two of A.A.'s Other "Founders"

1. **Professor William James**. In 1902, Professor William James wrote *The Varieties of Religious Experience*.[102] A.A.'s Big Book mentioned it at page 28. After Bill Wilson had his dramatic spiritual experience at Towns Hospital in New York, he read the James book in order to understand what had just happened to him. *Pass It On* related that Bill "now had his spiritual experience ratified by a Harvard professor, called by some *the* father of American psychology."[103] Bill later said William James "had been a founder of Alcoholics Anonymous."[104] James's description of "conversion" follows and was frequently quoted by spiritual writers, particularly Dr. Samuel Shoemaker. James wrote:

> To be converted, to be regenerated, to receive grace, to experience religion, to gain an assurance, are so many phrases which denote the process, gradual or sudden, by which a self hitherto divided, and consciously wrong inferior and unhappy, becomes unified and consciously right, superior and happy, in consequence of its firmer hold upon religious realities.[105]

James might have been the source of the phrase "higher power," which AAs began to use in later years. For James wrote, "we are saved from the wrongness by making proper connection with the

---

[102] William James, *The Varieties of Religious Experience* (New York: New American Library, 1958). *DR. BOB* mentions the James book at page 306, stating, "The book, though not popular among Akron AAs, was a favorite of Dr. Bob's." Pittman's *AA The Way It Began* says, at page 197, that it was part of Dr. Bob's "Required Reading List."

[103] *Pass It On* (Alcoholics Anonymous World Services, Inc., 1984), pp. 124-25.

[104] *Pass It On*, p. 124.

[105] James, *The Varieties of Religious Experience*, p. 157. Shoemaker quotes this definition in his first book, *Realizing Religion*, at page 22. So does Howard A. Walter, *Soul Surgery* (Calcutta: Association Press, 1919), p. 119. See also Harold Begbie, *Twice-Born Men* (New York: Fleming H. Revell, 1909), pp. 16-17.

higher powers" (p. 383, *cf.* 99).[106] But James chose to call the supreme reality by the name of God—and AAs may have followed his lead in their Big Book. James wrote:

> God is the natural appellation, for us Christians at least, for the supreme reality, so I will call this higher part of the universe by the name of God (p. 389).

In any event, A.A.'s Big Book refers to James's book primarily to show there are "a multitude of ways in which men have discovered God" (Big Book, p. 28).

2. **Dr. Carl Jung**. A.A.'s Big Book also referred to Dr. Carl Jung and cited Jung as the source of A.A.'s "spiritual solution"—that the mind of a chronic alcoholic can only be healed by "vital spiritual experiences."[107] Years after the founding of A.A. in 1935, Bill Wilson wrote Dr. Carl Jung and said the concept of a spiritual or religious experience—in short, a genuine conversion—"proved to be the foundation of such success as Alcoholics Anonymous has since achieved."[108] And Dr. Bob seemed to have taken an interest in A.A.'s other "founder"—Dr. Carl Jung. For Dr. Bob owned and read Dr. Jung's book, *Modern Man in Search of a Soul.*[109] Jung wrote:

> Among all my patients in the second half of life—that is to say, over thirty-five—there has not been one whose problem in the last resort was not that of finding a religious outlook on life. It is safe to say that every one of them fell ill because he had lost that

---

[106] For a more likely Oxford Group source of the expression, "Higher Power," see the book by Bill Wilson's Oxford Group friend and writer, Victor C. Kitchen, *I Was A Pagan* (New York: Harper & Brothers, 1934), p. 85. For further discussion, see Dick B., *New Light on Alcoholism*, p. 87

[107] See Big Book, pp. 26-27.

[108] *Pass It On*, pp. 382-83.

[109] C. J. Jung, *Modern Man in Search of a Soul* (New York: Harcourt Brace Jovanovich, Publishers, 1933). Owned by family.

which the living religions of every age have given to their followers, and none of them has really been healed who did not regain his religious outlook (p. 264).

Authors of Special Interest to Dr. Bob

Various people have said that this or that author or book was a favorite of Dr. Bob's.[110] But we cannot state with any certainly which particular books were Dr. Bob's "favorites." We can and shall list below the authors of books most frequently mentioned by Dr. Bob, his wife, Anne, his family, and his co-workers. We also list those authors who, by the sheer number of their books that Dr. Bob owned, seem to have been favored in his reading.

1. **James Allen**.

A. *As a Man Thinketh*.[111] The title of this popular pamphlet was probably taken from the first part of Proverbs 23:7, "For as he thinketh in his heart, so *is* he." James Allen said:

Man is manacled only by himself: thought and action are the jailers of Fate—they imprison, being base; they are also the angels of Freedom—they liberate, being noble (p. 18).

Good thoughts and good actions can never produce bad results; bad thoughts and actions can never produce good results (p. 24).

---

[110] For example, Sue Smith Windows told the author that the Glenn Clark books were favorites. Dorothy S. M. said that Drummond's *The Greatest Thing in the World*, Emmet Fox's *The Sermon on the Mount*, and *The Upper Room* were the "three main books at that time" (*DR. BOB*, pp. 310-11). *DR. BOB* said William James' *The Varieties of Religious Experience* "was a favorite of Dr. Bob's" (p. 306). Pittman's *AA The Way It Began* said the Bible, Drummond's book, James's book, *The Upper Room*, and Russell's *For Sinners Only* constituted Dr. Bob's "required reading" (p. 197). In his memo to Lois Wilson, Bob E. mentioned Drummond, Fox, and James Allen's *As a Man Thinketh* as particularly important to Dr. Bob.

[111] James Allen, *As a Man Thinketh* (New York: Peter Pauper Press, Inc., n.d.). *RHS* mentions, p. 34. Bob E.'s List. Nell Wing's List in *AA The Way It Began*, p. 192.

Keep your hand firmly upon the helm of thought (p. 64).

B. *Heavenly Life*.[112]

2. **Harold Begbie**. Anne Smith's Journal mentioned two of Harold Begbie's many books. Dr. Bob read them both.

A. *Twice-Born Men*.[113] This earliest of Begbie's titles was written in 1909. Begbie said he wrote his book as a footnote in narrative to Professor James's *Varieties* "to bring home to men's minds this fact concerning conversion, that, whatever it may be, *conversion is the only means by which a radically bad person can be changed into a radically good person*" (p. 17). Begbie covered "new birth" and "born again." And he gave narrative examples.

B. *Life Changers*.[114] In this book, Dr. Frank Buchman, founder of the Oxford Group, was referred to throughout as "F. B." Begbie discussed almost every aspect of Oxford Group ideas which came into such prominence in the 1930's: (1) Sin (pp. 14-15). (2) Soul Surgery (pp. 24-41). (3) God Consciousness (p. 39). (4) Confession (p. 104). (5) The belief elements of Frank Buchman's "A First Century Christian Fellowship"—forerunner of the Oxford Group (p. 122). (6) The origin of Buchman's five C's—Confidence, Confession, Conviction, Conversion, and Continuance (pp. 169-70). (7) Quiet Time for prayer, Bible study, and "listening for the direction of the Holy Spirit" (pp. 169-70). (8) Sharing (p. 175).

---

[112] James Allen, *Heavenly Life* (New York: Grosset & Dunlap, n.d.). Owned by family.

[113] Harold Begbie, *Twice-Born Men* (New York: Fleming H. Revell, 1909).

[114] Harold Begbie, *Life Changers: Narratives of a Recent Movement in the Spirit of Personal Religion* (London: Mills & Boon, Limited, 1932). Owned by family.

3. **Oswald Chambers**.

A. *My Utmost for His Highest*. This particular daily Bible devotional by Chambers was in use by Dr. Bob, Anne Smith, Bill Wilson, Lois Wilson, and Henrietta Seiberling. It was also widely read by members of the Oxford Group. Bill Wilson's wife, Lois, specifically mentioned in her Oxford Group Notebook that she was reading this book and "really saw myself."[115] For further information, see our discussion under "Daily Bible Devotionals."

B. *Studies in the Sermon on the Mount*. Dr. Bob studied the Sermon on the Mount in the Bible itself (Matthew 5-7). And he fleshed out his study with books about Jesus's sermon by such men as Glenn Clark, Oswald Chambers, Emmet Fox, and E. Stanley Jones—none of whom was a "member" of the Oxford Group or connected with Dr. Samuel Shoemaker's Calvary Church. For further information, see our discussion under "The Sermon on the Mount."

4. **Glenn Clark**. Clark was a professor of English and also an athletic director at Macalester College in Minnesota. He gained fame as a writer of prayer books and as the founder of "The Camps Farthest Out," where there were meditations, prayers, discussions, talks on Jesus and other biblical topics, Bible study, singing, and quiet time.[116] As we have said, Dr. Bob's daughter said that Glenn Clark's books were favorites of Dr. Bob's; and his daughter-in-law said that Dr. Bob and Anne attended Clark's Camps Farthest Out.

A. *The Soul's Sincere Desire*.[117] Clark wrote this essay after what he termed God's blessing him over a period of three

---

[115] See discussion in Dick B., *The Akron Genesis of Alcoholics Anonymous*, p. 151.

[116] See Clark's autobiography, *A Man's Reach*.

[117] Glenn Clark, *The Soul's Sincere Desire* (Boston: Little, Brown, 1925). Owned by family.

years "with an almost continuous stream of answered prayer." This, he said, resulted in a "peace and happiness and absolute liberation from the bondage of fear and anger and the life-destroying emotions that came to me and revealed to me the practicability of finding the Kingdom of Heaven in the practical world of men" (p. 3). His book was written to demonstrate "how you pray" (p. 4). He used the Lord's Prayer and the Twenty-third Psalm as a frame for prayer. Dr. Bob and Henrietta Seiberling favored this book; and so, apparently, did early AAs since it was one of the ten books A.A.'s first archivist said they read.[118]

B. *Fishers of Men.*[119] Clark wrote this book to answer the question, how to save men. Clark was not a "member" of the Oxford Group, but quoted many of its evangelical sources, such as Henry Drummond, John Mott, and H. A. Walter. Clark proposed an attitude described in the New Testament record of the Good Samaritan. He said, "I have faith that the man's need may be met, I have faith in God's power to meet it, I have faith that the love I have for the man may furnish a channel for the bringing of the need and the power together" (p. 4). Clark's Bibliography is of special interest because it recommended a good many of the books Dr. Bob read. Because of the early date of this Glenn Clark book, in relation to Dr. Bob's search, and because of the popularity of all Glenn Clark's books with Dr. Bob, his wife, Henrietta Seiberling, and early AAs, we wonder—without knowing—whether Dr. Bob's library and reading list were in fact influenced by the Clark's recommendations in the bibliography of *Fishers of Men.*

C. *I Will Lift Up Mine Eyes.*[120] Clark based this book on a story about "hind's feet"—taken from 2 Samuel 22:34—"He maketh my feet like hind's *feet*: and setteth me upon my high

---

[118] See Pittman, *AA The Way It Began*, p. 192.

[119] Glenn Clark, *Fishers of Men*. (Boston: Little, Brown, 1928). Owned by family.

[120] Glenn Clark, *I Will Lift Up Mine Eyes* (New York: Harper & Brothers, 1937). Owned by family.

places." This verse contains a figure of speech concerning the deftness and accuracy with which a mother deer tests the difficult spots on a mountain, finds the safe path, and then places both sets of her feet in precisely the same spot to enable a safe journey for herself and the baby deer. A friend said to Clark, "All you have to do is to make your feet like hind's feet and God will do the rest." The friend continued, "First, something happens inside one. Get that? Inside one—deep, deep down inside one." He then said, "[H]ere is the miraculous part that you will find hard to believe—after the change happens inside, everything begins to change *outside* too" (p. 2—italics in original). After that introduction to his topic, Clark discussed a number of key phrases which may also have arrested Dr. Bob's attention. The expressions included: (1) Jesus' statement, "Have Faith in God," (2) "As a man thinketh in his heart, so is he," and (3) "The tongue can no man tame."[121]

Clark proposed some prayer studies which he called "leaders." The studies were based on the Lord's Prayer and on the following in Philippians 4:8:

> Finally, brethren, whatsoever things are true, whatsoever things *are* honest, whatsoever things *are* just, whatsoever things *are* pure, whatsoever things *are* lovely, whatsoever things *are* of good report; if *there be* any virtue, and if *there be* any praise, think on these things.

---

[121] Compare the parallel interests: (1) Faith: Clark ("Have faith in God," p. 11); Dr. Bob ("As long as people have faith and believe" - *RHS*, p. 28); (2) As a man thinketh: Clark ("As a man thinketh," p. 11); Dr. Bob ("As a man thinketh," *RHS*, p. 34); (3) The tongue: Clark ("the tongue can no man tame," p. 14); Dr. Bob ("guard that erring member the tongue," *DR. BOB*, p. 338). Of course, one cannot say Dr. Bob got these Biblical ideas and phrases only from Glenn Clark; but there is a remarkable degree of similarity between the ideas Clark wrote about and those which attracted Dr. Bob's specific attention.

D. *Two or Three Gathered Together.*[122] Clark took this title from Matthew 18:20, where Jesus said, "For where two or three are gathered together in my name, there am I in the midst of them." Clark mentioned the names of many of the Christian leaders of prayer who were to become important in Dr. Bob's reading—E. Stanley Jones, Harry Emerson Fosdick, Sherwood Eddy, and Rufus Jones. Clark had received a letter from Toyohiko Kagawa—another of Dr. Bob's favorites—proposing that prayer become the spearhead for a Kingdom of God Movement in America and the world. And Clark described that movement, which involved the men we mentioned and several others. According to Clark, all believed there is special power when two or more Christians are gathered together in prayer. Their starting point was Jesus's declaration in the Sermon on the Mount, "Seek ye first the kingdom of God." And the Movement was to give itself three definite, distinct forms of expression: (1) The Quiet Hour for cultivating the vital experience of God in each individual heart. (2) The Prayer Group for cultivating the expression of vital, cooperative prayer with others. (3) The opening of avenues for bringing the strength and inspiration of the Quiet Hour and of the Prayer Group into vital, constructive expression in the social movements of the day. Recommending something that may also be referred to in the Big Book's Eleventh Step discussion, Clark said:

> With people who are new to the discipline of deepening the prayer life, it is often well to use the first half or two-thirds of the time for study centered around some book. Merely reading aloud *The Practice of the Presence of God* by Brother Lawrence for the first half hour will do wonders in lifting a group into the attitude and spirit of true prayer (p. 73).[123]

---

[122] Glenn Clark, *Two or Three Gathered Together* (New York: Harper & Brothers, 1942). Owned by family.

[123] Compare Big Book, p. 87: "If circumstances warrant, we ask our wives or friends to join us in morning meditation."

Clark then listed many of the authors and books that Dr. Bob read and that we have covered in this book.[124]

E. *How to Find Health through Prayer.*[125] Clark believed healing necessitated removal of *particular* blockages to God—selfishness, anger, fear—and then prayer for healing (pp. 29-37). Clark said it was not the prayer that created the miracle, but the healing state of consciousness that prayer induces. He said: (1) "The best way to induce it is to live daily practicing the presence of God" (p. 79), and then (2) "Turn off hate and fear and self and turn on Faith and Hope and Love," in so doing, he said, you "step into the Secret Place of the Most High where all healing power abides" (p. 79). His meditations used Bible verses such as "underneath are the everlasting arms" [Deuteronomy 33:27].

F. *The Man Who Talks with Flowers.*[126]

G. *Clear Horizons.*[127]

H. *The Lord's Prayer and Other Talks on Prayer from The Camps Farthest Out.* See also our discussion under "Prayer."

I. *God's Reach.*[128]

---

[124] On pages 74-75, Clark specifically mentioned Drummond, Heard, Starr Daily, E. Stanley Jones, Fosdick, Weatherhead, *Tertium Organum*, and Frank Laubach. Of Emmet Fox, Clark says, "and *The Sermon on the Mount* by Emmet Fox to those who lean toward New Thought" (p. 74).

[125] Glenn Clark, *How to Find Health through Prayer* (New York: Harper & Brothers, 1940). Owned by family.

[126] Glenn Clark, *The Man Who Talks with Flowers* (Minnesota: Macalester Park Publishing Company, 1939). Owned by family.

[127] A bound quarterly, volume 2 (St. Paul: Macalester Park Publishing Company, 1941). Glenn Clark, editor. Owned by family.

[128] Glenn Clark, *God's Reach* (MN: Macalester Park Publishing, n.d.). Owned by family.

    J. *Touchdowns for the Lord: The Story of "Dad" A. J. Elliott.*[129]

5. **Lloyd Douglas**. Dr. Bob owned a good many books by Lloyd Douglas, who was a Christian minister in an Akron Church in the 1930's. The books are all still owned by Dr. Bob's family. We will not detail them because most involve fiction, but we have listed them in the footnote.[130]

6. **Henry Drummond**.

    A. *The Greatest Thing in the World*. See our discussion under "Love."

    B. *Natural Law in the Spiritual World.*[131]

7. **Harry Emerson Fosdick**. Fosdick, the famous pastor of Riverside Church in New York, had more than a passing impact on A.A., both before and after the Big Book was completed.[132] His endorsement of A.A. is included in the Big Book at page 574. Dr. Bob owned and read a good many Fosdick books long before the publication of the Big Book, and even before A.A. So did Dr. Bob's wife, Anne. The following are some of their Fosdick books:

---

[129] Glenn Clark, *Touchdowns for the Lord: The Story of "Dad" A. J. Elliott.* (Minnesota: Macalester Park Publishing Co., 1947).

[130] Lloyd Douglas, *The Robe* (Mass: Houghton Mifflin, 1942); *The Big Fisherman* (Mass: Houghton Mifflin, 1948); *White Banners* (N.Y.: Grosset & Dunlop, 1936); *Green Light* (N. Y.: Houghton Mifflin, 1935); *Forgive Us Our Trespasses* (N. Y.: Grosset & Dunlop, 1932).

[131] Henry Drummond, *Natural Law in the Spiritual World* (New York: John B. Alden, 1887). Owned by family.

[132] See the discussion of Fosdick in Mel B., *New Wine*, pp. 143-47, 153.

A. *The Meaning of Service.*[133] Fosdick said:

> One of the most inveterate and ruinous ideas in the history of human thought is that neither service to man nor any moral righteousness whatsoever is essential to religion. In wide areas of religious life, to satisfy God has been one thing, to live in righteous and helpful human relations has been another (p. 1).
> . . . *[T]he inevitable expression of real Christianity is a life of sacrificial service* (p. 18, italics in original).

Fosdick commented on verse after verse in the New Testament to show the New Testament emphasis on service. After one series of Bible quotes, Fosdick said, "Read these verses and observe one thing: the Master's earnest desire to share with his disciples the best blessings he had. His peace, his love, his joy—he did not wish to keep them to himself. . . . *Before we can fully enjoy anything we must share it*" (pp. 56-57, italics in original). He concluded his book with a chapter, titled "The Motive of Gratitude," saying:

> The distinguishing quality of the Christian motive for unselfishness lies here: *we are expected to live sacrificial lives, because we ourselves are the beneficiaries of sacrificial living beyond our power to equal or repay* (pp. 194-95, italics in original).

B. *The Meaning of Prayer.*[134] For further information, see our discussion in "Prayer."

---

[133] Harry Emerson Fosdick, *The Meaning of Service* (London: Student Christian Movement, 1921). Owned by family.

[134] Harry Emerson Fosdick, *The Meaning of Prayer*. (New York: Association Press, 1926). Anne Smith mentions. Glenn Clark recommended this book for the "Morning Watch" in *Fishers of Men* (p. 98).

C. *The Manhood of the Master.*[135] This book was arranged for daily and weekly Bible studies on topics pertaining to Jesus's ministry.

D. *As I See Religion.*[136] Fosdick viewed genuine religion as inward communion from which come peace and power.

E. *On Being a Real Person.*[137] Fosdick wrote this book on personal counseling. He said:

> Without exaggeration it can be said that frustrated, disintegrated, inhibited, unhappy people, who cannot match themselves with life and become efficient personalities, constitute the greatest single tragedy in the world (p. 3).

Fosdick's thesis was that we must shoulder responsibility for ourselves. He said, "Life consists not simply in what heredity and environment do to us but in what we make out of what they do to us" (p. 5). Fosdick said, "Jesus is reported to have said to Peter when Peter asked about another man's lot, 'What is that to thee? follow thou me.' . . . Peter accepts Peter, with his distinctive and restricted endowment, and will see now what can be made of *that*" (p. 59). Writing on the practical use of faith, Fosdick said:

> No man can really become an unbeliever; he is psychologically shut up to the necessity of believing—in God, for example, or else in no God, or else in the impossibility of deciding. One way or another, in every realm, man is inherently a believer in something or other, positive or negative, good or bad, or indifferent (pp. 240-41).

---

[135] Harry Emerson Fosdick, *The Manhood of the Master* (London: Student Christian Movement, 1924). Anne Smith mentions.

[136] Harry Emerson Fosdick, *As I See Religion* (New York: Grossett & Dunlap, 1932). Owned by family.

[137] Harry Emerson Fosdick, *On Being a Real Person* (New York: Harper & Brothers, 1943). Owned by family.

Fosdick concluded:

> A constructive faith is thus the supreme organizer of life, and, lacking it, like Humpty Dumpty we fall and break to pieces, and the wonder is whether all the king's horses and all the king's men can ever put us together again (p. 264).

F. *A Great Time to Be Alive.*[138]

G. *The Man from Nazareth.*[139] Fosdick wove the story of Jesus's ministry in terms of the way Jesus was seen by his contemporaries.

8. **Emmet Fox**. We leave to evaluation by others just how much influence Emmet Fox had on A.A. The matter has certainly been discussed in recent writings.[140] One author, Mel B., stated, "Bill Wilson freely acknowledged the importance of the book (Fox's *The Sermon on the Mount*) to A.A." (p. 111). But such acknowledgments do not appear in any of A.A.'s official histories such as *AA Comes of Age, Pass It On,* or *DR. BOB and the Good Oldtimers.* Igor Sikorsky, Jr., asserted that Emmet Fox was one of "A.A.'s Godparents," but Sikorsky's book contains no documentation of the asserted close relationship between Fox and A.A.[141] Emmet Fox was not connected with the Oxford Group or Sam Shoemaker, to whom Bill Wilson attributed A.A.'s ideas; and Fox, in fact, wrote a good deal about what he claimed was the

---

[138] Harry Emerson Fosdick, *A Great Time to Be Alive* (New York: Harper Brothers, 1944). Owned by family.

[139] Harry Emerson Fosdick, *The Man from Nazareth: As His Contemporaries Saw Him* (New York: Harper & Brothers, 1949). Owned by family.

[140] See, for example, Mel B., *New Wine*, pp. 5, 105-06, 111-14.

[141] See Igor I. Sikorsky, Jr., *AA's Godparents: Carl Jung, Emmet Fox, Jack Alexander* (Minnesota: CompCare Publishers, 1990).

mythology of certain Biblical concepts such as sin and atonement.[142]

But the sin and atonement concepts were very much a part of the belief system of the Oxford Group and of Shoemaker. Whatever conflict there may be between the views of Oxford Group writers and Fox as to the Bible, the fact is that Dr. Bob did read and recommend Fox's *The Sermon on the Mount*. And Dr. Bob owned and read several other Fox books and pamphlets. Anne Smith did not mention Fox or his ideas in her Journal. But Nell Wing listed Fox's *The Sermon on the Mount* as among ten books she believed "Early AAs Read."[143] The following Fox books were a part of Dr. Bob's collection:

A. *The Sermon on the Mount*.[144] *AA The Way It Began* did not include this book on Dr. Bob's "Required Reading List." *DR. BOB* mentioned it at pages 310-11, attributing to Dorothy S. M. the statement that Dr. Bob got her the book. Dorothy said there were three main books of her time, namely, *The Upper Room* (actually a periodical), Drummond's *The Greatest Thing in the World*, and Fox's *The Sermon on the Mount*. See also *DR. BOB* at page 151, which, again quoting Dorothy S. M., said: "Many remember that 'The Sermon on the Mount,' by Emmet Fox, was also very popular." In any event, Dr. Bob owned it and read it, and the book is still in his family's possession.

B. *Find and Use Your Inner Power*.[145]

---

[142] Emmet Fox, *The Sermon on the Mount* (New York: Harper & Row, 1934), pp. 4-5, 7-8.

[143] Pittman, *AA The Way It Began*, p. 192.

[144] Fox, *The Sermon on the Mount*. On Bob E.'s list.

[145] Emmet Fox, *Find and Use Your Inner Power* (New York: Harper & Brothers, 1937). Owned by family.

C. *Power through Constructive Thinking*.[146]

D. *Alter Your Life*.[147]

E. *Emmet Fox pamphlets*. The following Fox pamphlets are owned by Dr. Bob's family: *Getting Results by Prayer* (1933), *You Must Be Born Again* (1936), *The Great Adventure* (1937), and *Your Heart's Desire* (1937).

9. **E. Stanley Jones**. This leading American religious figure during A.A.'s founding years has been much overlooked in A.A. histories. Bill Wilson apparently never mentioned E. Stanley Jones; yet a copy of Jones's *Along the Indian Road* is among the few A.A. source books at Bill Wilson's home at Stepping Stones.[148] Glenn Clark frequently mentioned Jones.[149] So did the Reverend Sam Shoemaker. Former Congressman John Seiberling informed the author that his mother, Henrietta Seiberling, owned and read a number of E. Stanley Jones books.[150] In writing about guided reading, Anne Smith stated in her Journal, "all of E. Stanley Jones' books are very good."[151] Sue Smith Windows, Dr. Bob's daughter, told the author her father read a number of the Jones books.[152] And today Dr. Bob's family still owns several of E. Stanley Jones' books. They are:

---

[146] Emmet Fox, *Power through Constructive Thinking* (New York: Harper & Brothers, 1932). Owned by family.

[147] Emmet Fox, *Alter Your Life* (New York: Harper, 1950). Owned by family.

[148] During his visit to Stepping Stones at Bedford Hills, New York, in October, 1991, the author located a copy of this book in the upstairs library of the Wilson home.

[149] See, for example, Clark, *One Man's Reach*, 276-78; *Two or Three Gathered Together*, p. 74; *Fishers of Men*, p. 97.

[150] Letter to the author from John F. Seiberling, dated August 14, 1991.

[151] See Dick B., *Anne Smith's Journal*, p. 82. (The statement quoted in the text will be found on pages 16 and 48 of the Journal itself—these page numbers being those which were assigned to the Journal copy in the possession of A.A.'s General Services Archives in New York).

[152] Interview with Sue Windows, Founders Day Conference, in June, 1991.

A. *The Christ of the Mount.*[153] See our discussion under "The Sermon on the Mount."

B. *Along the Indian Road.*[154]

C. *Abundant Living.*[155] Many of the book's topics—how to find God, self-centeredness, resentments, fear, and guidance—are familiar to AAs.

D. *Victorious Living.* See our discussion under "Daily Bible Devotionals."

E. *Other E. Stanley Jones books.* There were several other E. Stanley Jones books of the era prior to the Big Book's publication of which Anne Smith spoke indirectly in her Journal when she lauded "all of E. Stanley Jones' books." Sue Smith Windows wrote the author that all the books Anne mentioned were read by Dr. Bob. We do not know if any of the Jones books mentioned in the next footnote was *not* read. But we set forth in our footnote some important Jones books of the time.[156]

10. **Toyohiko Kagawa**. Dr. Bob spoke frequently of God as a God of love.[157] So did his wife, Anne.[158] And though Dr. Bob

---

[153] E. Stanley Jones, *The Christ of the Mount* (New York: The Abingdon Press, 1931).

[154] E. Stanley Jones, *Along the Indian Road* (New York: Abingdon Press, 1939).

[155] E. Stanley Jones, *Abundant Living.* (New York: Abingdon-Cokesbury Press, 1942).

[156] E. Stanley Jones, *The Christ of the Indian Road (New York: Abingdon Press, 1925); Christ at the Round Table* (New York: The Abingdon Press, 1928); *The Christ of Every Road* (New York: The Abingdon Press, 1930); *Christ and Human Suffering* (New York: The Abingdon Pres, 1933); *The Choice Before Us* (New York: The Abingdon Press, 1937); *The Christ of the American Road* (New York: Abingdon-Cokesbury Press, 1944); *Way to Power & Poise* (New York: Abingdon Press, 1949).

[157] *DR. BOB*, p. 110.

owned and read Kagawa's book on love; and though the discussion of it occupied four pages of Anne Smith's Journal; and though Kagawa is frequently mentioned by the other writers, such as Clark and Jones; neither he nor his book, *Love: The Law of Life*, has surfaced in A.A. histories.[159] Kagawa, a Christian pastor, wrote no fewer than five books on the Christian religion. These books contained his interpretation, from different aspects, of the significance of Jesus. *Love* is a study of a great many ingredients of Christian love. Kagawa stated, "The love of Christ stands out as the greatest thing known to humanity" (p. 37).

11. **Charles M. Sheldon**. Sheldon, a young Christian minister in Topeka, Kansas, wrote *In His Steps* and read it to his congregation. The book has reportedly sold 30 million copies since its publication in 1897. The opening question in the book was, "What would Jesus do?" The theme verse was 1 Peter 2:21: "For even hereunto were ye called; because Christ also suffered for us, leaving us an example, that ye should follow his steps."[160]

Religion and the Mind

One could characterize the following books as having to do with the "mental" or "psychological" aspects of Dr. Bob's spiritual quest. But they also cover more general discussions of religion:

---

[158] (...continued)

[158] *DR. BOB*, p. 117; Kurtz, *Not-God*, p. 55. In her signed statement for the author, dated June 8, 1991, Sue Windows stated on page 2, "Mother often used the expression, 'God is love.'"

[159] Toyohiko Kagawa, *Love: The Law of Life* (Philadelphia: The John C. Winston Company, 1929). Owned by family.

[160] Charles M. Sheldon, *In His Steps* (Pennsylvania: Whitaker House, 1979). See the recommendation of this book by Glenn Clark in *Fishers of Men*, p. 97. Henrietta Seiberling's daughter, Dorothy Seiberling, wrote the author on August 14, 1991, that Henrietta had read *In His Steps*. Owned by family.

1. *In Tune with the Infinite* by Ralph Waldo Trine.[161] Often quoting Scripture, Trine aimed at perfect peace. He wrote:

> This is the Spirit of Infinite Peace, and the moment we come into harmony with it there comes to us an inflowing tide of peace, for peace is harmony. A deep interior meaning underlies the great truth, "To be spiritually minded is life and peace." To recognize the fact that we are spirit, and to live in this thought, is to be spiritually minded, and so to be in harmony and peace (p. 135).

> We need more faith in every-day life—faith in the power that works for good, faith in the Infinite God, and hence faith in ourselves created in His image (p. 147).[162]

> A knowledge of the Spiritual Power working in and through us as well as in and through all things, a power that works for righteousness, leads to optimism. . . . He it is who realizes the truth of the injunction, "Rest in the Lord, wait patiently for Him and He shall give thee thy heart's desire" (pp. 148-49).

> In the degree, then, that we work in conjunction with the Supreme Power do we need the less to concern ourselves about results (p. 149).

William James discussed Trine's writing at some length in his *The Varieties of Religious Experience*.[163] And, as we've already mentioned, James's book was important to both Bill W. and Dr. Bob.

---

[161] Ralph Waldo Trine, *In Tune with the Infinite* (New York: Thomas Y. Crowell, 1897). Owned by family,

[162] Compare the following language in the Big Book at page 68, "we are now on a different basis, the basis of trusting and relying upon God. We trust infinite God rather than our finite selves. . . . Just to the extent that we do as we think He would have us, and humbly rely on Him, does He enable us to match calamity with serenity."

[163] See James, *The Varieties of Religious Experience*, pp. 93, 302.

2. *The Man Who Knew* by Ralph Waldo Trine.[164]

3. *Modern Man in Search of a Soul* by Dr. Carl G. Jung. See discussion under A.A.'s "Founders."[165]

4. *Peace of Mind* by Joshua Loth Liebman.[166] Dr. Bob proclaimed:

> We're all after the same thing, and that's happiness. We want peace of mind. The trouble with us alcoholics was this: We demanded that the world give us happiness and peace of mind in just the particular way we wanted to get it—by the alcohol route. And we weren't successful. But when we take time to find out some of the spiritual laws, and familiarize ourselves with them, and put them into practice, then we do get happiness and peace of mind (*DR. BOB*, p. 308).

Bill Wilson made a special gift of Liebman's book to Dr. Bob.[167]

5. *Psychology of a Christian Personality* by Ernest M. Ligon.[168] Ligon examined Christian personality from the standpoint of the Sermon on the Mount.

---

[164] Ralph Waldo Trine, *The Man Who Knew* (New York: Bobbs Merrill, 1936). Owned by family.

[165] Dr. Carl G. Jung, *Modern Man in Search of a Soul* (New York: Harcourt, Brace and Company, 1933). Owned by family. See Mel B., *New Wine*, page 15.

[166] Joshua Loth Liebman, *Peace of Mind* (New York: Simon & Schuster, 1946). Owned by family.

[167] Bill's inscription—which the author has inspected—reads, "To Smitty - my wonderful friend of AA. Bill, Xmas '46." Owned by family.

[168] Ernest M. Ligon, *Psychology of a Christian Personality* (New York: Macmillan, 1935). Owned by family.

6. *Religion Says You Can* by Dilworth Lupton.[169] The Reverend Dr. Dilworth Lupton was the pastor of Cleveland's First Unitarian Church and played a role in the growth of A.A. in Cleveland, once the Cleveland AAs had severed their Oxford Group connection in Akron, Ohio.[170] Lupton wrote:

At the heart of this book's message is my personal faith that religion, more than any other human experience, can help a man so re-create his character and personality that he can stand like a rock against adversity. By religion I do not mean church-going lip service to creeds—I mean rather that amazing awareness that men have felt through the ages that they were of "finer stuff than the stars" (p. ix).

The truly religious man, of whatever faith, possesses a third line of defense. He finds power not only in himself and in his friends and affections: he also draws on the power of God. . . . Christian religion is one of the most valuable and potent influences that we have for producing that harmony and peace of mind and that confidence of soul which is needed to bring health (pp. 80-81).

7. *The Rediscovery of Man* by Dr. Henry C. Link.[171] Link focused on psychology, which, he said, is a study of habits and their formation. He stated that habits acquired by practice make a mind, thinking, and reasoning. He believed that psychology has rediscovered man and the powers of which he is capable when his mind has been freed from prevailing fallacies about himself. He believed that *personality* is an attribute and defines the extent to which the individual has developed habits and skills which interest and serve other people. He believed that the Christian concept of personality does not stop with the process of service, of loving

---

[169] Dilworth Lupton, *Religion Says You Can* (Boston: The Beacon Press, 1938). Owned by family.

[170] For a discussion of Lupton's role, see Kurtz, *Not-God*, pp. 84-85.

[171] Henry C. Link, *The Rediscovery of Man* (New York: Macmillan, 1939). Owned by family.

one's neighbor, or being one's brother's keeper. All of these aspects of personality are rediscovered in the concept of obedience to moral law. He believed Christ is the great liberator in the world today and inspires man to achieve his highest personality under Christ's codes.

Quiet Time

Dr. Bob owned a book on Quiet Time, titled, *The Quiet Time*, written by S. D. Gordon.[172]

We will mention several other titles as part of this Quiet Time category. All were well known Oxford Group books of the 1920's and 1930's, and specifically addressed the topic of Quiet Time. It seems likely they were read by Dr. Bob, Anne, Henrietta, and T. Henry and Clarace Williams. All these people made Quiet Time the focus of their prayer and meditation life. Their Quiet Time involved Bible study, two-way prayer (praying to God and listening for guidance from God), writing down the leading thoughts received, and utilizing devotionals and other Christian literature to aid their study and thinking process. The Oxford Group Quiet Time books are:

1. *The Guidance of God* by Eleanor Napier Forde.[173]
2. *When Man Listens* by Cecil Rose.[174]
3. *The Quiet Time* by Howard J. Rose.[175] This Oxford Group pamphlet outlined the Quiet Time procedure and contained the verses of Scripture that pertain to it.

---

[172] S. D. Gordon, *The Quiet Time* (London: Fleming, n.d.). Owned by family.

[173] Eleanor Napier Forde, *The Guidance of God* (Oxford: Printed at the University Press, 1930). Portions of Miss Forde's comments appear to have been quoted by Anne Smith in her Journal; and Anne mentions Eleanor Forde by name in the Journal.

[174] Cecil Rose, *When Man Listens* (New York: Oxford University Press, 1937).

[175] Howard J. Rose, *The Quiet Time* (New York: Oxford Group at 61 Gramercy Park North, 1937).

4. *God Does Guide Us* by W. E. Sangster.[176]

5. *The God Who Speaks* by Burnett Hillman Streeter.[177]

6. *What Is The Oxford Group?* by The Layman with a Notebook.

7. *How Do I Begin?* by Hallen Viney.[178] This little pamphlet is a primer on how to receive and write down leading thoughts from God.

8. *Vital Touch with God: How to Carry on Adequate Devotional Life* by Jack C. Winslow.[179]

9. *When I Awake* by Jack C. Winslow.[180]

10. *How to Find Reality in Your Morning Devotions* by Donald W. Carruthers.[181] Though Carruthers was apparently not a "member" of the Oxford Group, his pamphlet was much recommended by Dr. Samuel Moor Shoemaker and was frequently used by Oxford Group people.

Miscellaneous

In describing the foregoing books, we endeavored to categorize them in such a way that the reader could identify either the authors or the subjects that seemed most to interest Dr. Bob in his spiritual quest. But there are still other books that were read and studied by Dr. Bob. We list them under "Miscellaneous," not to denigrate them, but rather because they do not particularly fit in the lists

---

[176] W. E. Sangster, *God Does Guide Us* (New York: The Abingdon Press, 1934).

[177] Burnett Hillman Streeter, *The God Who Speaks* (New York: The Macmillan Co., 1936).

[178] Hallen Viney, *How Do I Begin?* (New York: The Oxford Group at 61 Gramercy Park, 1937).

[179] Jack C. Winslow, *Vital Touch with God: How to Carry on Adequate Devotional Life*, Reprint of an article in *The Calvary Evangel*, n.d.

[180] Jack C. Winslow, *When I Awake* (London: Hodder & Stoughton, 1938).

[181] Donald W. Carruthers, *How to Find Reality in Your Morning Devotions* (Pennsylvania State College, n.d.)

above. The following are some additional books that Dr. Bob owned and read. All are in the possession of his family:

1. *The Art of Living* by Norman Vincent Peale.[182]
2. *The Art of Selfishness* by David Seabury.[183] Seabury suggested that man master and obey two great principles: (1) The Basic Law of Being—*never compromise yourself.* (2) The Magic Formula of Human Relations—*no ego satisfactions* (pp. 4-5). Seabury concluded his book with long lists of what he called evil selfishness and good selfishness. Examples of the evil forms were fear, anger, sex lust, and egotism; and of the contrasting good forms: caution, courage, elation, and tolerance (pp. 244-45).
3. *The Basic Thoughts of Confucius* by Miles Menander Dawson.[184]
4. *The Basic Teachings of Confucius* by Miles Menander Dawson.[185]
5. *Drinking's Not the Problem* by Charles Clapp, Jr.[186]
6. *The Greatest Story Ever Told* by Fulton Oursler.[187]
7. *Happy Grotto* by Fulton Oursler.[188]
8. *How to Win Friends and Influence People* by Dale Carnegie.[189]
9. *The Initiate* by his Pupil.[190]

---

[182] Norman Vincent Peale, *The Art of Living* (New York: Abingdon Press, 1937).

[183] David Seabury, *The Art of Selfishness* (New York: Pocket Books, 1974). *DR. BOB* mentions, p. 310.

[184] Miles Menander Dawson, *The Basic Thoughts of Confucius* (New York: Garden City Publishing Co., 1939).

[185] Miles Menander Dawson, *The Basic Teachings of Confucius* (Brandon Publishing Co., n.d.).

[186] Charles Clapp, Jr., *Drinking's Not the Problem* (Thom Y. Cromwell, 1949).

[187] Fulton Oursler, *The Greatest Story Ever Told* (New York: Doubleday, 1949).

[188] Fulton Oursler, *Happy Grotto* (Declan & McMullen, 1948).

[189] Dale Carnegie, *How to Win Friends and Influence People* (New York: Simon & Schuster, 1937).

[190] The Initiate by his Pupil (London: George Rontledge & Sons, 1944).

10. *Kingdom Come* by Ivan Cooke.[191]

11. *Lead Kindly Light* by Vincent Sheean.[192]

12. *Life Abundant for You* by Louise B. Brownell.[193]

13. *Outline of Modern Occultism* by Cyril Scott.[194]

14. *Parish the Healer* by Maurice Barbanelle.[195]

15. *Peace of Soul* by Fulton J. Sheen.[196] A major aspect of Sheen's book concerns the peace that comes from finding God.

16. *Perfect Everything* by J. R. Moseley.[197]

17. *Quiet Talks with The Master* by Eva B. Werber.[198]

18. *The Razor's Edge* by W. Somerset Maugham.[199]

19. *Rose Dawn* by Stewart Edward White.[200]

20. *The Secrets of the Saints* by Henri Gheon.[201]

21. *Sign at Six* by Stewart Edward White.[202]

22. *Song of Bernadette* by Franz Werfel.[203]

---

[191] Ivan Cooke, *Kingdom Come* (London: Wright & Brown Furnell, n.d.).

[192] Vincent Sheean, *Lead Kindly Light* (New York: Random House, 1949).

[193] Louise B. Brownell, *Life Abundant for You* (Aquarian Ministry, 1928).

[194] Cyril Scott, *Outline of Modern Occultism* (Dale News, 1935). This is one of several books Dr. Bob read on spiritualism and psychic phenomena. When the author visited Bill Wilson's home at Stepping Stones, he found a huge number of similar books in a room to the right of the entrance to the Stepping Stones home. A.A.'s Conference Approved biography of Wilson mentions this type of literature and Bill Wilson's "spook sessions." See *Pass It On* (New York: Alcoholics Anonymous World Services, 1984), pp. 275-80. A.A.'s Conference Approved biography of Dr. Bob indicates that Dr. Bob and some others in his area also became involved in psychic activities. But the biography makes clear that "Doc backed off,". . . that "[t]hey felt it might be dangerous," and that Akron AAs "were all against this spiritualist thing." See *DR. BOB*, pp. 311-13.

[195] Maurice Barbanelle, *Parish the Healer* (London: Ebenezer Baylis, 1941).

[196] Fulton J. Sheen, *Peace of Soul* (New York: McGraw Hill, 1949).

[197] J. R. Moseley, *Perfect Everything* (MN: Macalester, n.d.).

[198] Eva B. Werber, *Quiet Talks with The Master* (Marina Del Rey, California: DeVorss, 1936).

[199] W. Somerset Maugham, *The Razor's Edge* (New York: Doubleday, 1944).

[200] Stewart Edward White, *Rose Dawn* (Doubleday Page, 1920).

[201] Henri Gheon, *The Secrets of the Saints* (New York: Longman's Green, 1929).

[202] Stewart Edward White, *Sign at Six* (New York: Bobbs Merrill, 1912).

[203] Franz Werfel, *Song of Bernadette* (New York: Viking Press, 1942).

23. *Teachings of the Temple.*[204]
24. *Tertium Organum* by Peter D. Uspenskii.[205]
25. *The Unknown God* by Alfred Noyes.[206]

The Weatherhead Puzzle

Where is Leslie D. Weatherhead? An important name that is missing from A.A. histories and from our list of Dr. Bob's books is that of Dr. Leslie D. Weatherhead. Weatherhead was mentioned in passing by Glenn Clark.[207] But we have included this discussion on Weatherhead because of his close connection with the Oxford Group in the 1930's, and the fact that two of his books—with Henrietta Seiberling's name written in them—are linked to Bill Wilson's scanty library of Biblical materials.[208]

Weatherhead's *Discipleship* is located in the upstairs library at Bill Wilson's home at Stepping Stones in New York.[209] The book contains a virtual manual on Oxford Group principles and practices that found their way into A.A. Its chapters include: (1) Surrender, (2) Sharing, (3) The Quiet Time, (4) Fellowship, (5) Guidance, (6) The Will of God, (7) Restitution, and (8) Witness. Did Dr. Bob read it? We just don't know. Bill Wilson's former secretary, Nell Wing, owns another Weatherhead book,

---

[204] *Teachings of the Temple* (Temple of the People Publishing, 1925).

[205] Peter D. Uspenskii, *Tertium Organum* (New York: A.A. Knopf, 1922). *DR. BOB* mentions, p. 310. Recommended by Glenn Clark in *Fishers of Men*.

[206] Alfred Noyes, *The Unknown God* ((New York: Sheed & Ward, 1940).

[207] See Clark, *Two or Three Gathered Together*, p. 74.

[208] Leslie D. Weatherhead, Ph,D., D.D., was Minister Emeritus of The City Temple, London, and formerly President of the Methodist Conference in Great Britain. He authored some twenty-five titles.

[209] Leslie D. Weatherhead, *Discipleship* (New York: The Abingdon Press, 1934). The author inspected this book at Stepping Stones and found Henrietta's name written in it. Henrietta's daughter, Dorothy Seiberling, had told the author that many of Henrietta's books had been sent to A.A. This may have been one. In any event, it wound up at Bill's home at Bedford Hills, New York.

Psychology and Life.[210] This book is inscribed with Henrietta Seiberling's name and was a present from Bill to Nell. We also mention here Weatherhead's *How Can I Find God?*.[211]

Weatherhead's books dealt with a challenge, also tendered in the Big Book: Find God now![212] Henrietta Seiberling read Weatherhead, and Henrietta was much involved in the early spiritual education of Dr. Bob and Bill W. Weatherhead's books are on target as to the Oxford Group principles that influenced Bob and Bill. And we believe they might well have formed a part of Dr. Bob's reading, or, at least, the ideas from Weatherhead that Henrietta may have imparted to Dr. Bob.

The Calvary Evangel List of Oxford Group Literature

There are a great many books by Oxford Group people and about the Oxford Group that were written in the 1930's and thereafter.[213] For several reasons we have not previously listed them.

We have found no evidence to date that Bill Wilson had more than two or three Oxford Group books in his possession in the 1930's; and we have found none by Dr. Samuel Shoemaker—to whom Bill attributed most of the Steps. We have not yet tracked down more than six Oxford Group books that Henrietta Seiberling owned and read. And they are in our list of books that Dr. Bob

---

[210] Leslie D. Weatherhead, *Psychology and Life* (New York: Abingdon Press, 1935).

[211] Leslie D. Weatherhead, *How Can I Find God?* (New York: Fleming H. Revell, 1934). We did not find this among Bill Wilson's or Dr. Bob's books.

[212] The Big Book's actual language, on page 59, states: "But there is One who has all power—that One is God. May you find Him now!"

[213] See Dick B., *The Oxford Group & Alcoholics Anonymous*, pp. 378-88; *The Books Early AAs Read for Spiritual Growth*, 7th ed. (Kihei, HI: Paradise Research Publications, 1998); and *New Light on Alcoholism*, pp. 353-59.

read.[214] Similarly, we have not seen more than eight Oxford Group books and five Sam Shoemaker books that Dr. Bob owned and which are still owned by his family. And we have listed these. We have also listed other Oxford Group-Shoemaker books mentioned by Anne Smith and known to have been read by her husband.

But these previously listed books may not include a good many Oxford Group books of the 1930's which Henrietta Seiberling probably read. They also may not include all of what Dr. Bob described as the "immense" number of books recommended to him by the Oxford Group. To be sure our readers know all the Oxford Group books which were probably read by Dr. Bob, we include here the entirety of the books listed as Oxford Group literature in *The Calvary Evangel*. In our first edition, we mentioned only those specified in the March, 1939, issue of *The Evangel*. But we have now added additional books, recommended in pre-1939 issues of *The Evangel*, which we located during our 1993 visit to the Calvary Church archives in New York.[215] The following books and pamphlets were recommended by *The Calvary Evangel* which was the "house organ" of the Oxford Group in America. It therefore seems very likely that these books found their way into Dr. Bob's hands, either through Henrietta Seiberling, through T. Henry and Clarace Williams, through the literature stocked in the furnace room at the Williams' home in Akron, or through other Oxford Group sources with whom Dr. Bob and his wife were in contact during the years they belonged to the Oxford Group between 1933 and 1939.

---

[214] The Oxford Group books known to have been read by Henrietta Seiberling, and our sources of information about that fact, are: (1) *Life Changers* by Harold Begbie (John Seiberling's letter to the author, dated August 14, 1991); (2) *For Sinners Only* by A. J. Russell (J. Seiberling letter, 8/14/91); (3) *Soul Surgery* by H. A. Walter (J. Seiberling letter, 8/14/91) (4) *Inspired Children* by Olive M. Jones (Dorothy Seiberling's letter to the author, dated July 19, 1991); (5) *If I Be Lifted Up* by Samuel M. Shoemaker (J. Seiberling letter, 8/14/91); (6) *Children of the Second Birth* by Samuel M. Shoemaker (Dorothy Seiberling's letter to the author, dated August 14, 1991).

[215] See Dick B., *New Light on Alcoholism*, pp. 347-51.

As they were listed in 1935-1939 issues of *The Calvary Evangel*, the following Oxford Group books were recommended:

1. *Inspired Youth* by Olive Jones.[216]
2. *For Sinners Only* by A. J. Russell.[217]
3. *I Was a Pagan* by V. C. Kitchen.[218]
4. *Life Began Yesterday* by Stephen Foot.[219]
5. *The Church Can Save the World* by S. M. Shoemaker.[220]
6. *The God Who Speaks* by B. H. Streeter.[221]
7. *Children of the Second Birth* by S. M. Shoemaker.[222]
8. *Twice-Born Ministers* by S. M. Shoemaker.[223]
9. *If I Be Lifted Up* by S. M. Shoemaker.[224]
10. *Confident Faith* by S. M. Shoemaker.[225]
11. *The Gospel According to You* by S. M. Shoemaker.[226]
12. *Inspired Children* by Olive Jones.[227]
13. *What Is The Oxford Group?* by The Layman with a Notebook.[228]

---

[216] Olive Jones, *Inspired Youth* (New York: Harper & Brothers, 1938).

[217] A. J. Russell, *For Sinners Only* (London: Hodder & Stoughton, 1932).

[218] V. C. Kitchen, *I Was a Pagan* (New York: Harper & Brothers, 1934).

[219] Stephen Foot, *Life Began Yesterday* (New York: Harper & Brothers, 1935).

[220] Samuel M. Shoemaker, *The Church Can Save the World* (New York: Harper & Brothers, 1938).

[221] Burnett Hillman Streeter, *The God Who Speaks* (New York: The Macmillan Company, 1936).

[222] Samuel M. Shoemaker, *Children of the Second Birth* (New York: Fleming H. Revell, 1927).

[223] Samuel M. Shoemaker, *Twice-Born Ministers* (New York: Fleming H. Revell, 1929).

[224] Samuel M. Shoemaker, *If I Be Lifted Up* (New York: Fleming H. Revell, 1931).

[225] Samuel M. Shoemaker, *Confident Faith* (New York: Fleming H. Revell, 1932).

[226] Samuel M. Shoemaker, *The Gospel According to You* (New York: Fleming H. Revell, 1934).

[227] Olive Jones, *Inspired Children* (New York: Harper & Brothers, 1933).

[228] The Layman with a Notebook, *What Is The Oxford Group?* (London: Oxford University Press, 1933).

14. *Religion That Works* by S. M. Shoemaker.[229]
15. *The Conversion of the Church* by S. M. Shoemaker.[230]
16. *National Awakening* by S. M. Shoemaker.[231]
17. *The Venture of Belief* by Philip M. Brown.[232]
18. *Realizing Religion* by S. M. Shoemaker.[233]
19. *Church in Action* by Jack Winslow.[234]
20. *Why I Believe in the Oxford Group* by Jack Winslow.[235]
21. *Soul Surgery* by Howard Walter.[236]
22. *When Man Listens* by Cecil Rose.[237]
23. *The Guidance of God* by Eleanor Napier Forde.[238]
24. *New Leadership* by Garth Lean and Morris Martin.[239]
25. *New Enlistment* by Wilfred Holmes-Walker.[240]

---

[229] Samuel M. Shoemaker, *Religion That Works* (New York: Fleming H. Revell, 1928).

[230] Samuel M. Shoemaker, *The Conversion of the Church* (New York: Fleming H. Revell, 1932).

[231] Samuel M. Shoemaker, *National Awakening* (New York: Harper & Brothers, 1936).

[232] Philip M. Brown, *The Venture of Belief* (New York: Fleming H. Revell, 1935).

[233] Samuel M. Shoemaker, *Realizing Religion* (New York: Association Press, 1923).

[234] Though we have made an extensive search for this book, and for information about it, we have not been able to obtain any information. We asked Oxford Group offices in the United States and in the United Kingdom. We have also made inquiry of long-time Oxford Group activists in the United States and abroad, and of Shoemaker associates, all to no avail.

[235] Jack C. Winslow, *Why I Believe in the Oxford Group* (London: Hodder & Stoughton, 1934).

[236] Howard A. Walter, *Soul Surgery: Some Thoughts on Incisive Personal Work*, 6th ed. (Oxford at the University Press by John Johnson, 1940). 1st ed. published 1919).

[237] Cecil Rose, *When Man Listens* (New York: Oxford University Press, 1937).

[238] Eleanor Napier Forde, *The Guidance of God* (Oxford, The Oxford Group, printed at the University Press by John Johnson, 1930).

[239] Garth Lean and Morris Martin, *New Leadership* (London: Wm. Heinemann, Ltd., 1936).

[240] Wilfrid Holmes-Walker, *New Enlistment* (London: The Oxford Group, circa 1937).

26. *How Do I Begin* by Hallen Viney.[241]

27. *The Quiet Time* by Howard Rose.[242]

28. *How to Find Reality in Your Morning Devotions* by Donald Carruthers.[243]

29. *The Person of Christ* by L. W. Grensted.[244]

30. *Calvary Church in Action* by John Potter Cuyler, Jr.[245]

31. *Seeking and Finding* by Ebenezer Macmillan.[246] This is one of the very few Oxford Group books the author found in Bill Wilson's library at Stepping Stones, Bedford Hills, New York.

32. *Christ's Words from the Cross* by Samuel M. Shoemaker.[247]

As we have previously mentioned, a number of new books were located at The Episcopal Church Archives and are set forth in Appendix 2.

Healing

As the second edition of this title was going to press, we located three books on healing which were read by Dr. Bob and were owned by his family. None had been mentioned in any A.A. literature we had seen. Nor had we been able to inspect the books themselves.

We knew only that Dr. Bob had a great interest in the importance of prayer, that he prayed for others, and that he

---

[241] Hallen Viney, *How Do I Begin?* (New York: Oxford Group at 61 Gramercy Park, North, 1937).

[242] Howard J. Rose, *The Quiet Time* (Sussex: Howard J. Rose, 6 The Green, Slaugham, Haywards Heath, n.d.).

[243] Donald W. Carruthers, *How to Find Reality in Your Morning Devotions* (Pennsylvania State College, n.d.).

[244] L. W. Grensted, *The Person of Christ* (New York: Harper & Brothers, 1933).

[245] John Potter Cuyler, Jr., *Calvary Church in Action* (New York: Fleming H. Revell, 1934).

[246] Ebenezer Macmillan, *Seeking and Finding* (New York: Harper & Brothers, 1933).

[247] Samuel M. Shoemaker, Jr., *Christ's Words from the Cross* (New York: Fleming H. Revell, 1933).

believed that God could heal. We have now read the three books, and reflected on the other healing books Dr. Bob had read. These, of course, included books by Mary Baker Eddy and by Unity writers, as well as those by Starr Daily, Frank Laubach, Glenn Clark, and several others.

However, these three books go right to the heart of Christian healing as Dr. Bob was studying it. The books are:

1. *Christian Healing* by Charles Filmore.[248]

2. *Healing in Jesus' Name* by Ethel R. Willitts.[249] The evangelist takes as her text Exodus 15:26: "I am the Lord that healeth thee." She expresses the hope that her series of sermons which she believed came to her by revelation, "might enable thousands of suffering people to partake of these blessings that are in the Bible." Her first sermon deals with the necessity for salvation by following the gospel of Romans 10:9. She points to healings described in the Bible and to people she had seen healed through reading the Word of God. She covered the will of God that all classes of people be healed. She covered the fact that *all* diseases were healed by Jesus when he was on earth. She covered stumbling blocks to faith. And she also pointed to James 5:14, which was a healing guide also used by early AAs at the time of their surrenders. She covered the importance of overcoming fear through belief in what the Bible says to the effect "that we can be healed." She pointed out that believers are complete in Jesus Christ (Colossians 2:9-10)-"delivered from all sin and sickness." She pointed particularly to the statement that by "his [Christ's] stripes

---

[248] Charles Filmore, *Christian Healing* (Kansas City: Unity School of Christianity, 1936).

[249] Ethel R. Willitts, *Healing in Jesus' Name* (Detroit: Ethel R. Willitts, Evangelist, 1931).

we are healed [which was the prophecy in Isaiah 53:5].[250] Willitts stressed her view that salvation and healing are united in the Bible. Much of her book is devoted to her own experiences with healing.

3. *Heal the Sick* by James Moore Hickson.[251]

As we have already covered, Glenn Clark was one of Dr. Bob's favorite authors. In 1927, Glenn Clark's *The Soul's Sincere Desire* swept the nation in popularity. And it arrested the attention of Henrietta Seiberling, Dr. Bob, Anne Smith, and early AAs. Two chapters in that book are significant here. The first is titled "A Lost Art of Jesus" and deals with Jesus's statement: "He that believeth on me, the works that I do shall he do also; and greater works than these shall he do; because I go unto my Father."[252] The other chapter is titled "In His Name." Clark points out that seven different times Jesus gave his disciples a promise the purport of which was, "whatsoever ye shall ask of the Father in my name, he may give it you."[253]

---

[250] Jesus's accomplishments were expressed in 1 Peter 2:24: ". . . by whose [Christ's] stripes ye were healed."

[251] James Moore Hickson, *Heal the Sick* (London: Methuen & Co., 1925).

[252] See John 14:12.

[253] See John 15:16.

4

What's New?

New Materials in This Revised Edition

Since the publication of our First Edition, a number of new resources have been located. Over the past years of research and writing, we have received many phone calls and letters from those who are following our historical quest.

They have wanted to know if there were any books that Dr. Bob owned, in addition to those previously listed. And there are. They have asked if there were Oxford Group books that were read by Dr. Bob and the Akron AAs, in addition to those listed in *Dr. Bob's Library*, *Anne Smith's Journal*, and *The Oxford Group & Alcoholics Anonymous*. And there are. They have asked if there were books by Dr. Sam Shoemaker that might have influenced AAs and that were not been listed in *The Akron Genesis of Alcoholics Anonymous*, *The Books Early AAs Read for Spiritual Growth*, and *New Light on Alcoholism: The A.A. Legacy from Sam Shoemaker*. And there are. They have asked what new information we have found about the Daily Devotionals that were used in early A. A. Quiet Times; and they have asked how those devotionals were used. And there is now substantial information accumulated on that subject, much of which appears in our title, *Good Morning!: Quiet Time, Morning Watch, Meditation, and Early A.A.* And they have asked for more specifics as to what Dr. Bob and the early AAs were studying in the Bible, particularly in the Sermon on the Mount (Matthew 5-7), the Lord's Prayer (Matthew 6:9-13), 1 Corinthians 13, and the Book of James. Some of these answers will appear in the next chapter. Many appear in our title, *The Good Book & The Big Book: A.A.'s Roots in the Bible*.

The new books we have found are sandwiched in appropriate categories in our previous chapter. But many AAs, clergy, substance abuse workers, recovery centers, and historians are using our materials for further work. Others are collecting books. So we will list here those titles which have been added in this revised edition and which form a part of the books Dr. Bob read (or at least probably read) and recommended.

First, there are Dr. Bob's books that were owned by his family and located among their effects after the First Edition had been published. Publishing and other specific data on these books appear in the previous chapter. These are the new titles we have discovered: Harry Emerson Fosdick's *The Man from Nazareth* and *The Manhood of the Master*; Charles Whitney Silkey's *Jesus and Our Generation*; Glenn Clark's *The Lord's Prayer and Other Talks on Prayer from The Camps Farthest Out*; *God's Reach*; and *Touchdowns for the Lord: The Story of "Dad" A. J. Elliott*; James Allen's *Heavenly Life*; Professor Henry Drummond's *Natural Law in the Spiritual World*; Norman Vincent Peale's *The Art of Living*; R. Llewelyn Williams's *God's Great Plan, a Guide to the Bible*; Charles M. Layman's *A Primer of Prayer*; F. L. Rawson's *The Nature of True Prayer*; James Moore Hickson's *Heal the Sick*; Charles Filmore's *Christian Healing*; Ethel Willitts's *Healing in Jesus Name*; Ralph Waldo Trine's *The Man Who Knew*; S. D. Gordon's *The Quiet Time*; and *The Fathers of the Church*.

Second, there are Oxford Group and Calvary Church book-room titles we have since located: (1) through the libraries of, and contacts with, Oxford Group people; (2) at the Calvary Church archives in New York; (3) The Episcopal Church Archives in Austin, Texas; and (4) in various writings about Oxford Group literature. These are the recently found titles: Samuel M. Shoemaker's *How to Help People*; *A First Century Christian*

Fellowship: A Defense of So-Called Buchmanism by One of Its Leaders; *My Life-Work and My Will*; John Potter Cuyler, Jr.'s *Calvary Church in Action*; H. W. "Bunny" Austin's *Moral Re-Armament: The Battle for Peace*; David Blair's *For Tomorrow-Yes!*; Charles Clapp, Jr.'s *Drinking's Not the Problem*; L. W. Grensted's *The Person of Christ*; Irving Harris's *An Outline of the Life of Christ*; Amelia S. Reynold's *New Lives for Old*; J. H. Smith's *The Meaning of Conversion*; Donald W. Carruthers's *How to Find Reality in Your Morning Devotions*; and Ebenezer Macmillan's *Seeking and Finding*.

Next, there are the many books by E. Stanley Jones, which were popular with Dr. Bob, with Anne Smith, and with Henrietta Seiberling. Those not previously mentioned are: *Christ at the Round Table*, *The Christ of the Indian Road*, *The Christ of the American Road*, *Way to Power and Poise*, and *Abundant Living*.

One can find other titles written by authors mentioned above. But we have limited the Dr. Bob Library list of new additions to those books which fell into A.A. hands, or which are mentioned or were used by those people and those sources with whom the early AAs—particularly Dr. Bob—were in actual contact.

The Search Goes On

The author has devoted much of his time and research, and many of his interviews and inquiries, to learning what AAs studied in the Bible. We believed, for a long time, that Dr. Bob's books held a major key. But recently we have taken a different approach. We have attempted to learn what Oxford Group people themselves, particularly Frank Buchman, were actually teaching from the Bible during the 1930's, and at their meetings and houseparties. The assumption was and is that Dr. Bob, Anne Smith, Henrietta Seiberling, T. Henry and Clarace Williams, and Bill Wilson necessarily would have been exposed to this material both through the books they read, and through the Oxford Group gatherings themselves. Hence, when we learned that there were at least three major Oxford Group writers who had assembled Biblical teachings from the talks, views, and writings of Frank Buchman, we considered these writing sources of great importance and value.

The first source is Miles G. W. Phillimore. His importance as an exponent of Frank Buchman's Biblical teachings and views, during A.A.'s formative years in the 1930's, has been confirmed to us by: (1) Michael Hutchinson--a resident of Oxford in the United Kingdom, an Oxford Group activist since the early 1930's, and a close associate of Garth Lean, biographer of Dr. Frank N. D. Buchman, founder of the Oxford Group. (2) Dr. Morris Martin--long-time personal secretary to, and colleague of, Buchman.[1] (3) George Vondermuhll, Jr.--an Oxford Group activist for over forty years, and the former corporate secretary of the Oxford Group's American entity, Moral Re-Armament. (4) Reverend T. Willard Hunter--author, columnist, platform orator, friend of A.A. and of Frank Buchman, and long-time Oxford Group volunteer.

Miles Phillimore was a son of an English Lord. When he met the Oxford Group, his father told him he must either sever his connection with it or leave Cambridge University. Phillimore chose to leave. He was sent to farm in New Zealand, where people were changed through him. When he came back to England, he spent time at the home of the parents of Michael Hutchinson and later became Michael's friend. Phillimore was closely associated with the Oxford Group from the early 1930's until Buchman's death in 1961.

In 1940, Buchman gathered a team of Oxford Group people at Lake Tahoe, California. The scene was a Cross, formed of snow-

---

[1] Dr. Morris Hugh Martin is a scholar, author, and educator. He was born in London, England, the son of missionaries. He received his Ph.D. from Oxford, and has lived in many countries of the world. He has been involved with *Up With People* since its inception. He was Dean of Faculty at Mackinac College from 1965-1969. He served on the Adjunct Faculty at the University of Hartford and the University of Arizona from 1973 to 1977. He was a Visiting Professor and Lecturer at Princeton University, 1973-1976. He is the author of *The Thunder and the Sunshine* (Washington, D.C.: Moral Re-Armament, n.d.) and *Born to Live in the Future*. He was a close personal associate of Dr. Frank N. D. Buchman for many years.

filled rock crevices on the face of Mount Tallac. At that time, Phillimore assembled and wrote *Just for Today*. It was a privately printed pamphlet made up of sentences, hymns, and passages often quoted by Buchman when revealing the core of his passionate faith. *Just for Today* sets forth the heart of many of Buchman's Bible teachings and thoughts. Hutchinson and Vondermuhll each provided the author with copies of this pamphlet.

Dr. Bob and Anne Smith, Henrietta Seiberling, and T. Henry and Clarace Williams, in Akron, Ohio--as well as Bill and Lois Wilson, and their Oxford Group friends, on the East Coast--were all in touch with Buchman's ideas through Oxford Group meetings and houseparties, and through personal conversations. And Phillimore's presentations in 1940, which catalogued Buchman's earlier Bible teachings, seem very likely to represent the Biblical concepts A.A.'s founders had been hearing since 1933.

Phillimore's *Just for Today* covered Psalm 103; 1 John 1:7; Ephesians 3:20-21; Psalm 23; and Romans 12. It also contained a good many *expressions* which were taken from Bible verses.

The second source for Buchman's Biblical teachings is Reverend Harry J. Almond, a minister of the Reformed Church in America. That Almond's writings faithfully portrayed Buchman's Biblical ideas has been confirmed to the author by Michael Hutchinson and George Vondermuhll, Jr. And it was Willard Hunter who first supplied the author with Almond's books and put the author in touch with Almond himself. Almond has been most communicative to the author, both as to his own work and as to the relevance of the other sources (Phillimore and Hicks) which we here discuss.

Since 1951, Almond has given his time to the world program of Moral Re-Armament. He presently serves as a member of its Board in the United States. In 1975, Moral Re-Armament published a pamphlet, compiled by Reverend Almond, titled *Foundations for Faith*. The pamphlet was revised and published in 1980 by Grosvenor Books. In his preface, Almond expressed a particular debt to Miles G. W. Phillimore. Before his death, Phillimore gave Almond permission to use material in Phillimore's

Just for Today. Almond also credited Roland W. Wilson's *The Old Testament for Modern Explorers* and Canon B. H. Streeter's *The God Who Speaks* (a book which was abridged by Roger Hicks--the third source discussed below).

Almond said he wrote *Foundations for Faith* to help people find answers to such questions as (1) "What is God like?" (2) "How can I live the way I should?" (3) "I try to read the Bible in the morning, and I know many people get so much from it; but, honestly, I often fall asleep trying to understand. What can I do?"

For answers, Almond offered the materials Buchman and the Oxford Group taught on a wide variety of Oxford Group Biblical subjects.

The Oxford Group said that man's basic problem is "sin." Almond pointed to those things the Bible calls "sin." They included the Ten Commandments (Exodus 20:2-17 and Deuteronomy 5:6-21). Then Jesus's teachings in Mark 7:20-23 and Matthew 5:19 and following. Then the problems defined in 1 Corinthians 6:9-11; Galatians 5:19-24; Colossians 3:5-10; and Romans 1:18-2:11. Almond then contrasted with the sin problems the standard of perfection in the Sermon on the Mount (Matthew 5:48) and the Biblical sources of the moral standards, honesty, purity, unselfishness, and love—the Oxford Group's Four Absolutes.

For the Biblical answers as to what to do about sin, Almond used Buchman/Shoemaker language, saying, "Hate it. Quit it. Cut it out." He pointed to basic verses on confession (Proverbs 28:13; James 5:16; 1 John 1:9-10), honesty with another (Psalm 51 and Psalm 32:3-5), and restitution (Luke 19).

Almond then pointed to verses which showed "Christ—the Cure." They were Romans 7:15-8:3; Romans 8:11; John 3:17; Matthew 11:28-29; Romans 10:13; Matthew 1:18-2:12; and Luke 2:1-20. Almond pointed to verses on the resurrection of Christ and the victory achieved by him (1 Corinthians 15 and 1 Corinthians 3:11).

For the result—a miracle, Almond cited Hebrews 12:1-2; John 14:16, 26; and 16:7-15. There are a host of other specific Bible authorities for the life-changing process involving faith. And in our opinion, Almond's careful work contains a crucial historical tool for those who wish to see the Biblical foundations for the life-changing process of the Oxford Group, and the Biblical ideas which Dr. Bob, Anne Smith, Bill Wilson, and the other early AAs may have been studying in the Oxford Group literature and meetings, to which they referred.

On a recent visit to Fort Myers Beach, Florida, Eleanor Forde Newton (who is, perhaps, the oldest living Oxford Group activist, and was a good friend to Frank Buchman and Sam Shoemaker) handed us a book titled, *Creative Prayer*, by E. Herman. At first, we thought it was simply a book that Ellie used in her daily Quiet Times. We have since discovered that it was one of the popular Oxford Group books of the early days. It deals with prayer, the "ministry of silence," the discipline of meditation, "from self to God," the path to power, the apostolate of prayer, and the "priesthood of prayer."

Our final new information source is Roger Hicks. Once again, the faithfulness of Hicks as a source which accurately presented Buchman's Biblical concepts was confirmed to the author by: (1) Michael Hutchinson; (2) George Vondermuhll, Jr.; and (3) Dr. Morris Martin.

Hicks took his M.A. at Oxford. Then he taught history at Madras University. Later he studied theology at Westcott House, Cambridge. And his writings about the Bible and Biblical ideas have been favorites in the Oxford Group.

Hicks was connected with the Oxford Group from the mid-Twenties until Buchman's death in 1961. We have just begun to tap this rich historical resource. But we here call attention to the following titles by Hicks: (1) *The Endless Adventure.*[2] (2) *The*

---

[2] Roger Hicks, *The Endless Adventure* (London: Blandford Press, 1964).

Lord's Prayer and Modern Man.[3] (3) *Letters to Parsi.*[4] and (4) *How to Read the Bible: Notes for Revolutionaries.*[5]

The author recently learned some vital historical facts about Hicks. For one thing, Hicks was part of the Oxford Group team which joined Dr. Frank Buchman in Akron, Ohio, in January of 1933, when the famous team came there at the behest of Harvey Firestone to celebrate the recovery of Bud Firestone and to witness to the life-changing force of the Oxford Group program.

As has so often happened over the past several years, we delved into these new information sources because of suggestions and leads from the Reverend T. Willard Hunter. Hunter set in motion the process by which we obtained copies of the titles by Phillimore, Almond, and Hicks, and it was he who first called our attention to the significance and integrity of their writings.

---

[3] Roger Hicks, *The Lord's Prayer and Modern Man* (London: Blandford Press, 1967).

[4] Roger Hicks, *Letters to Parsi* (London: Blandford Press, 1950).

[5] Roger Hicks, *How to Read the Bible: Notes for Revolutionaries* (London: MRA, n.d.). The author recently received from the headquarters of The Oxford Group in Great Britain a copy of Howard A. Walter's *Soul Surgery*, which specified it was literature of "The Oxford Group." This sixth edition was printed at Oxford University Press in 1940. The back cover contained the statement that "The following books and pamphlets give information about the Oxford Group and Moral Re-Armament." Included in the recommended book list was *How to Read the Bible*. "Notes by Roger Hicks." Since the date was 1940, and since Hicks was active in the Oxford Group from the mid-1920's, was present with the famous Buchman team in Akron in 1933, and was writing his materials during this period, it seems possible that Dr. Bob, Anne, Henrietta, and the others in Akron might have heard Hicks or come into contact with his Biblical writing through Oxford Group recommendations. Hicks also edited Canon B. H. Streeter's *The God Who Speaks*, which was written in 1936, and was on Calvary Church's recommended list of Oxford Group books.

5

Dr. Bob's Biblical Sources Emerge

We are far from through with our effort to pin-point the specific places in the Bible from which Dr. Bob and the early AAs took their ideas. Oddly enough, though Dr. Bob was emphatic about, and precise in detail concerning, A.A.'s roots in the Bible, there are commentators who still seem to question A.A.'s Biblical roots.[1] But we believe the books Dr. Bob read, when coupled with

---

[1] See, for example, Charlie Bishop, Jr., & Bill Pittman, *To Be Continued: The Alcoholics Anonymous World Bibliography: 1935-1994* (WV: The Bishop of Books, 1994). Commenting on the first edition of *our* book (Item 716 in their book), the authors said, "The author [Dick B.] quotes Dr. Bob to the effect that AA's got the basic ideas for the Twelve Steps from their study of the Good Book, the Bible. That idea may be open to discussion but one certainly must credit Dick B. for extensive, original research into early A.A. history." Both Bishop and Pittman published early editions of our books, and we confess we cannot understand what is "open to discussion." As we have said before, *DR. BOB and the Good Oldtimers* quotes Dr. Bob as follows: (1) "They were convinced that the answer to their problems was in the Good Book." (2) "To some of us older ones, the parts that we found absolutely essential were the Sermon on the Mount, the 13th chapter of First Corinthians, and the Book of James." and (3) "We already had the basic ideas, though not in terse and tangible form. We got them . . . as a result of our study of the Good Book" (pp. 96-97). See also, *The Co-founders of Alcoholics Anonymous: Biographical sketches: Their last major talks* (New York: Alcoholics Anonymous World Services, 1972, 1975), pp. 9-10. One may quarrel with what we said about what Dr. Bob said, but we rest our point on the foregoing statements by Dr. Bob. To us, they do not seem "open to discussion." They do justify our quest for the basic ideas, both in the Bible and in the three portions of the Bible Dr. Bob cited.

the language we find in A.A. literature, are beacons in any quest for the Biblical ideas which influenced A.A.

Dr. Bob mentioned the Bible itself. He spoke of the Sermon on the Mount.[2] He spoke of 1 Corinthians 13. He, his wife (Anne), and Bill Wilson frequently alluded to, and quoted from, the Book of James. And even today, AAs often mention the Oxford Group's Four Absolutes—honesty, purity, unselfishness, and love—which derived exclusively from Christian teachings in the Bible. The Big Book itself, though supposedly "cleansed" of Biblical references, nonetheless contains quite a few. And the Biblical quotations and references in Anne Smith's Journal, as well as Henrietta Seiberling's frequent quotations from the Bible, also provide some very specific root sources for A.A.'s Biblical ideas.

Therefore, in this revised edition, we want to point to some Biblical ideas commonly found in A.A. and in the books Dr. Bob read. We can identify them with more certainty now than when we began our quest eight years ago.

We list below important Biblical words and expressions which have found their way, verbatim, into A.A.'s Big Book. In the footnotes, we document the location of the words and expressions in the Big Book, cite the Bible verse or verses which parallel the A.A. language, and then cite the book(s) in Dr. Bob's library in which the language can be found. The following are A.A. absorptions from the Bible:

Direct Biblical Quotations

1. Thy will be done.[3]
2. Thy will (not mine) be done.[4]

---

[2] So did Bill Wilson, as we have discussed.

[3] Big Book, pp. 67, 87, 443; Matthew 6:10; *What Is The Oxford Group?*, p. 48; Shoemaker, *Children of the Second Birth*, pp. 175-92.

[4] Big Book, p. 85; and compare "Thy will be done, not mine," pp. 229, 381; Luke 22:42 ("not my will, but thine, be done"); *What Is The Oxford Group?*, p. 48;

(continued...)

3. Love thy neighbor as thyself.[5]
4. Faith without works is dead.[6]
5. Creator.[7]
6. Maker.[8]
7. Father of Light.[9]
8. Father.[10]
9. Spirit.[11]
10. God.[12]
11. Restitution (Amends).[13]
12. Grudges.[14]

---

[4] (...continued)
Shoemaker, *Children of the Second Birth*, pp. 58, 182; Clark, *Soul's Sincere Desire*, p. 40.

[5] Big Book, pp. 153, 236; Leviticus 19:18; Matthew 19:19; 22:39; Mark 12:31; Romans 13:9; Galatians 5:14; James 2:8; (and compare Luke 10:27; and Matthew 5:43); Clark, *I Will Lift Up Mine Eyes*, p. 63; Holm, *The Runner's Bible*, pp. 27, 66; Tileston, *Daily Strength for Daily Needs*, p. 138.

[6] Big Book, pp. 14, 76, 88, 473; James 2:20, 26; (compare James 2:14, 17); *What Is The Oxford Group?*, p. 36.

[7] Big Book, pp. 13, 25, 28, 56, 68, 72, 75, 76, 80, 83, 158, 161; Isaiah 40:28; (compare Genesis 1:1); Begbie, *Life Changers*, p. 16; Brown, *The Venture of Belief*, p. 25.

[8] Big Book, pp. 57, 63, 525; Psalm 95:6. We found no correlative Oxford Group source; so Bill and Dr. Bob may have taken this directly from the Bible.

[9] Big Book, p. 14 [sic: Father of lights]; James 1:17; *The Runner's Bible*, p. 9.

[10] Big Book, p. 62; Matthew 5:45; Brown, *The Venture of Belief*, p. 25; Clark, *The Soul's Sincere Desire*, p. 9.

[11] Big Book, p. 46 ("the Realm of Spirit"); p. 66 ("the sunlight of the Spirit"); p. 84 ("the world of the Spirit"); p. 85 ("the flow of His Spirit into us"); p. 164 ("the Fellowship of the Spirit"); John 4:24; Holm, *The Runner's Bible*, pp. 16-19.

[12] Big Book (Over 200 specific references to God); Genesis 1:1; Begbie, *Life Changers*, p. 37.

[13] Big Book, pp. xvi, 292; Numbers 5:6-7; A. J. Russell, *For Sinners Only*, p. 119.

[14] Big Book, p. 65; James 5:9; Shoemaker, *Twice-Born Ministers*, p. 182.

13. Good Samaritan.[15]
14. God-sufficiency.[16]

Next come Biblical concepts, not all verbatim, which are firmly embedded in A.A., and have specific sources in the Bible and in Dr. Bob's books. In the footnotes, we list a reference to the expression in A.A. literature, then to the Biblical source(s), and finally to the book(s) in Dr. Bob's Library. The concepts are:

Recognizable Biblical Ideas

1. God is.[17]
2. God is love.[18]
3. Love ("Absolute Love").[19]
4. Honesty ("Absolute Honesty").[20]
5. Unselfishness ("Absolute Unselfishness").[21]

---

[15] Big Book, p. 97; Luke 10:33; Foot, *Life Began Yesterday*, pp. 177-80; Shoemaker, *Realizing Religion*, p. 80.

[16] Big Book, pp. 52-53; 2 Corinthians 3:5; 9:8; Shoemaker, *If I Be Lifted Up*, p. 107; Holm, *The Runner's Bible*, p. 138.

[17] Big Book, p. 53; Hebrews 11:6; Shoemaker, *The Gospel According to You*, p. 47; *Confident Faith*, p. 187.

[18] Dick B., *The Akron Genesis*, p. 121; *DR. BOB*, pp. 110, 116-17; Kurtz, *Not-God*, p. 55; 1 John 4:8, 16; Holm, *The Runner's Bible*, p. 6; Tileston, *Daily Strength for Daily Needs*, p. 139.

[19] Big Book, pp. 83-84, 88, 118; Matthew 5:43-46; 1 Corinthians 13; *Co-Founders*, p. 13; Helen Smith, *I Stand by the Door*, p. 24; *What Is The Oxford Group?*, pp. 107-08; Drummond, *The Greatest Thing in the World*.

[20] Big Book, pp. 13, 25, 28, 32, 45, 55, 57-58, 63-65, 67, 70, 73, 83, 145; *Pass It On*, p. 114; *The Language of the Heart*, p. 200; *Co-Founders*, p. 13; Matthew 5:33-37; Ephesians 4:25, 28; Philippians 4:8; *What Is The Oxford Group?*, pp. 74-83; Speer, *The Principles of Jesus*, p. 35; Wright, *The Will of God*, p. 187.

[21] Big Book, pp. xxv, 93, 127; *Co-Founders*, p. 13; Matthew 5:41-42; Matthew 16:24-26; Philippians 2:4-8; Foot, *Life Began Yesterday*; Shoemaker, *Realizing Religion*, p. 80; Speer, *The Principles of Jesus*, p. 35; Wright, *The Will of God*, p. 197.

6. Patience.[22]
7. Tolerance.[23]
8. Kindness.[24]
9. Forgiveness.[25]
10. Self-examination (Step 4).[26]
11. Admission of shortcomings or wrongs (Step 5).[27]
12. Setting things right with your brother (Steps 8, 9).[28]
13. Guidance of God (Step 11-"prayer and meditation").[29]
14. Witnessing (Step 12-"passing it on").[30]
15. Trust in God.[31]
16. Draw near to God, and He will draw near to you.[32]

---

[22] Big Book, pp. 67, 70, 83, 111, 118, 163; James 1:3-4; 5:7-11; Hebrews 10:36; Drummond, *The Greatest Thing in the World*.

[23] Big Book, pp. 19, 67, 70, 83-84, 118, 125; *Co-Founders*, pp. 4-5; 1 Corinthians 13; Drummond, *The Greatest Thing in the World*.

[24] Big Book, pp. 67, 83, 86; Ephesians 4:32; 1 Corinthians 13; Holm, *The Runner's Bible*, p. 66; Drummond, *The Greatest Thing in the World*.

[25] Big Book, pp. 77, 79, 86; Matthew 6:14-15; Luke 17:3-4; Colossians 3:13; Holm, *The Runner's Bible*, pp. 82-83, 88.

[26] Big Book, pp. 67, 69-70, 76, 84, 86, 98; Matthew 7:3-5; Chambers, *My Utmost for His Highest*, pp. 169, 174; Russell, *For Sinners Only*, pp. 309-16; Allen, *He That Cometh*, p. 140; Kitchen, *I Was A Pagan*, pp. 110-11.

[27] Big Book, pp. 72-73; James 5:16; *What Is The Oxford Group?*, p. 29; Shoemaker, *The Conversion of the Church*, p. 35.

[28] Steps Eight and Nine; *DR. BOB*, p. 308; Matthew 5:23-26; Russell, *For Sinners Only*, p. 120; Weatherhead, *Discipleship*, p. 113; Macmillan, *Seeking and Finding*, p. 176; Shoemaker, *The Conversion of the Church*, pp. 47-48; Holm, *The Runner's Bible*, p. 67; Chambers, *My Utmost for His Highest*, pp. 182-83.

[29] Dick B., *The Oxford Group*, pp. 230-57; *The Akron Genesis*, pp. 274-75; *New Light on Alcoholism*, pp. 315-16.

[30] See Dick B., *The Oxford Group & Alcoholics Anonymous*, pp. 290-95; *New Light on Alcoholism: The A. A. Legacy from Sam Shoemaker*, pp. 68, 317.

[31] Big Book, pp. 68, 98; Proverbs 3:5; Jeremiah 17:5-8; Holm, *The Runner's Bible*, pp. 41-45; *The Upper Room* for May 15, 1935; Tileston, *Daily Strength for Daily Needs*, pp. 37-108.

[32] Big Book, p. 57; James 4:8; *What Is The Oxford Group?*, p. 17; Chambers, *My Utmost for His Highest*, p. 309.

17. Humble yourself.[33]
18. Seek ye first the Kingdom of God.[34]

A.A. Slogans Adopted from Biblical Ideas

1. First Things First.[35]
2. One day at a time.[36]
3. The Grace of God.[37]
4. Easy Does It.[38]
5. Guard that erring member, the tongue.[39]

We are continuing our research and examination of A.A. ideas in terms of their roots in the Bible, Christian literature, and the Oxford Group. And we believe we shall find additional ideas that can be identified with a Biblical source that has been discussed by one or more writers of books Dr. Bob read.

The Point of the Quest for Sources

We believe the value of locating the Biblical roots of A.A. does not lie alone in finding out what Dr. Bob meant when he said AAs got their basic ideas from the Bible. Nor is the value merely from the excitement that comes when one learns the precise origin of

---

[33] Big Book, pp. 13, 57, 68; James 4:6, 10; 1 Peter 5:5, 6; Holm, *The Runner's Bible*, pp. 59, 81, 94.

[34] Big Book, p. 60; *DR. BOB and the Good Oldtimers*, p. 144; Dick B., *Anne Smith's Journal, 1933-1939*, p. 39; Matthew 6:33.

[35] Big Book, p. 135; *DR. BOB*, pp. 144, 192; Matthew 6:33; Macmillan, *Seeking and Finding*, p. 17.

[36] See Dick B., *The Akron Genesis*, p. 118; *Anne Smith's Journal*, p. 134; *DR. BOB*, p. 282; Matthew 6:34.

[37] Big Book, p. 25; Luke 2:40; Acts 11:23; Romans 5:15; 2 Corinthians 1:12; Dick B., *Anne Smith's Journal*, p. 24.

[38] Big Book, p. 135; Dick B., *The Akron Genesis*, p. 118; Matthew 6:34.

[39] James 3:1-13; *Co-Founders*, p. 5; *DR. BOB*, p. 338.

words he or she hears in Twelve Step meetings day after day, with
no explanation of their origin. There is a major purpose for
locating A.A.'s Biblical roots, a purpose recognizable in the Bible,
in Christian writings, and in A.A. itself.

In its simplest form, the purpose rests with the phrase, "Thy
will be done." To do the will of God is a major objective found in
the Bible, Christianity, and A.A.[40] So we necessarily ask what
the will of God is. Day after day in Twelve Step meetings people
pose the question: "What is God's will for me?"

The answers lie in the Word of God—the Good Book, as Dr.
Bob called it. "My son, if thou wilt receive my words . . . [t]hen
shalt thou understand the fear ["reverence"] of the Lord, and find
the knowledge of God," said the Old Testament.[41] "Thy word *is*
a lamp unto my feet, and a light unto my path," said Psalm
119:105.[42] "Thy will be done," said Jesus Christ.[43] "Thy word
is truth," said Jesus Christ.[44] "*Search the scriptures,*" said Jesus
Christ (emphasis added).[45] "All scripture *is* given by inspiration
of God," wrote the Apostle Paul (italics in original).[46] "Study to
shew thyself approved unto God . . . rightly dividing the word of
truth," wrote the Apostle Paul.[47]

A.A.'s Eleventh Step is directed solely at learning the will of
God and seeking the power to carry it out.[48] And Dr. Bob's
spiritual quest in literature pointed him unerringly toward the Good

---

[40] See, as to A.A., Big Book, 3rd ed., pp. 59, 63, 67, 88.

[41] Proverbs 2:1-5; See Fosdick, *The Meaning of Faith*, p. 30.

[42] See Holm, *The Runner's Bible*, pp. 128, 156.

[43] Matthew 6:10; Shoemaker, *Children of the Second Birth*, p. 187.

[44] John 17:17.

[45] John 5:39. See *The Upper Room* for August 12, 1938.

[46] 2 Timothy 3:16. For this foundational concept, Anne Smith cited 2 Peter 1:21 at
page 23 of her Journal (page number from A.A. General Service archives).

[47] 2 Timothy 2:15. See Tileston, *Daily Strength for Daily Needs*, p. 68; *The Upper
Room*, for April 27, and for September 30, 1938.

[48] Step Eleven: "Sought through prayer and meditation to improve our conscious
contact with God *as we understood Him*, praying only for the knowledge of His will for
us and the power to carry it out."

Book as the source of knowledge of God, God's will, and the power to carry out God's will.

Professor Henry B. Wright was the primary influence on the thinking of Dr. Frank Buchman, founder of the Oxford Group.[49] Wright wrote a major treatise on the will of God.[50] Wright's thesis was clear: The will of God could be learned from the Bible and from God's revelation to a person of His particular will for that person.

Sam Shoemaker frequently wrote that God's general or universal will could be found in the Bible.[51] Shoemaker also taught that God would reveal his particular will to a person if He (God) were asked, and if the person obeyed God's general or universal will.[52] Other Oxford Group writers also taught this concept.[53] Much of the study of the Bible by Dr. Bob, Anne, Henrietta, Bill, and the Akron AAs, as well as by their Oxford Group associates, was offering them all some very specific Biblical authority for their common solution (a conversion experience leading to a relationship with God) and the practical program of action that would make that experience possible. They sought God and God's will with the firm belief that if their relationship with God were right, great things would come to pass for them and countless others.[54] They called this the Great Fact.[55]

A study of Dr. Bob's reading discloses how they commenced their seeking and what the Bible taught about completing the search for God's will. And we believe the Biblical sources of A.A.

---

[49] Dick B., *The Oxford Group*, p. 67.

[50] Henry B. Wright, *The Will of God and a Man's Lifework* (New York: The Young Men's Christian Association, 1909).

[51] Shoemaker, *A Young Man's View of the Ministry*, p. 78; *Twice-Born Ministers*, pp. 184-85; *The Conversion of the Church*, pp. 49-50.

[52] See Shoemaker's favorite verse, John 7:17; and Shoemaker, *Christ and This Crisis*, p. 106; *Realizing Religion*, pp. 58-62.

[53] Rose, *When Man Listens*, p. 17; Forde, *The Guidance of God*.

[54] Big Book, p. 164.

[55] Big Book, p. 164.

are emerging from the study of Dr. Bob's reading, from a comparison of that reading with the Biblical concepts in the Big Book, and from locating the foundational verses in the Bible.

Piece by piece, a picture of God's will, as early AAs expressed it in the Big Book and the Twelve Steps, is emerging from Dr. Bob's Library. Many of the books he read expressed a reliance on the following promise in Proverbs 3:5-6:

> Trust in the Lord with all thine heart; and lean not unto thine own understanding. In all thy ways acknowledge him, and he shall direct thy paths.[56]

[56] See *The Upper Room* for May 15, 1935; Holm, *The Runner's Bible*, p. 126; Tileston, *Daily Strength for Daily Needs*, p. 31; Clark, *I Will Lift Up Mine Eyes*, p. 151; Brown, *The Venture of Belief*, p. 40; Streeter, *The God Who Speaks*, p. 191; Benson, *The Eight Points of The Oxford Group*, p. 81.

6

Some Final Thoughts

About Dr. Bob's Library

First, what *is* Dr. Bob's Library? It is not located in a single place—yet. In the First Edition, we listed those books still in possession of Dr. Bob's family. Since the writing of that edition, some of Dr. Bob's books have been donated to Dr. Bob's Home, at 855 Ardmore Avenue in Akron, Ohio, and are on display there. We have also listed all the books recommended or mentioned by Dr. Bob's wife, Anne Smith, in her Journal, and which Dr. Bob read. To our list, we added books mentioned in *DR. BOB*, in *RHS*, and by Bob E., an early Akron AA. We have included some Shoemaker pamphlets and made mention of a copy of *Soul Surgery*, all of which were stuffed in the copy of Anne Smith's Journal we inspected at Stepping Stones in New York. As a speculation, we included the principal Oxford Group books of Dr. Bob's time, books which he was likely to have read. We are certain we have not listed all the books Dr. Bob owned or read. For we limited our list to the spiritual area—with the exception of Dale Carnegie. Also, some of Dr. Bob's books apparently were given away by Emma K. at the time of Dr. Bob's death.[1] We have had the complete cooperation of the Smith family, and this revised edition represents our best effort to describe the contents of "Dr. Bob's Library."

About the Good Book, A.A., and His Library

We have been particularly interested in the relationship of the Good Book, and the books about it, to Alcoholics Anonymous. What can the contents of Dr. Bob's library tell us about this topic? An answer lies in the Big Book's Eleventh Step discussion of prayer, meditation, morning devotions, and spiritual growth through reading. It said:

> There are many helpful books also. Suggestions about these may be obtained from one's priest, minister, or rabbi. Be quick to see where religious people are right. Make use of what they offer (p. 87).

We believe that Big Book language hearkens back to the Quiet Time, Bible study, prayer, daily devotions, meditation, and reading practices of the early AAs, particularly those at A.A.'s birthplace in Akron, Ohio. And their practices produced great success!

Another answer as to our title's relevance to A.A. was provided by Dr. Bob's wife, Anne, in the context of her Christian beliefs. She said in her Journal:

> LET ALL YOUR READING BE GUIDED. What does God want me to read? A newly surrendered person is like a convalescent after an operation. He needs a carefully balanced diet of nourishing and easily assimilated food. Reading is an essential

---

[1] Emma K. and her husband lived with Dr. Bob at the time of his death. Emma was authorized, by Dr. Bob's family, to dispose of some of his books; and *DR. BOB* quotes her as saying, "I gave the spiritual books to my minister and the medical books to two young doctors he helped get started" (p. 310).

part of the Christian's diet. It is important that he read that which can be assimilated and will be nourishing. If you don't know what books to read, see some one who is surrendered and who is mature in the Groups (p. 16).

Why re-invent the wheel? Dr. Bob, Anne, and the early AAs did what they felt was "guided" reading and attained spiritual maturity. And their reading shows how they did it. Anne Smith summed up, "Of course the Bible ought to be the main source book of all."

About the Source of A.A. Ideas

What did Dr. Bob mean when he said AAs got the basic ideas for the Twelve Steps from their study of the Good Book (the Bible)? What ideas? The books in Dr. Bob's library show what early AAs were studying about the Bible and therefore indicate what they may have obtained *from* the Bible. See, particularly, Dick B., *The Good Book and The Big Book: A.A.'s Roots in the Bible*.

About Dr. Bob's Own Path

Bill Wilson often emphasized Dr. Bob's success record, stating:

> In this human laboratory, he [Dr. Bob] has proved that any alcoholic, not too mentally defective, can recover if he so desires. The possible recovery among such cases has suddenly been lifted from almost nil to at least 50 percent, which, quite aside from its social implications, is a medical result of the first magnitude. Though, as a means of our recovery, we all engage in the work, Dr. Smith has had more experience and has obtained better results than anyone else.[2]

---

[2] *DR. BOB*, p. 174. Bill Wilson was not the only one to highlight the phenomenal success *rate* AAs achieved in the earliest years. At page xx, the Big Book states: "Of alcoholics who came to A.A. and really tried, 50% got sober at once and remained that

(continued...)

Years later, Bill added:

> . . . [Dr. Bob] had treated 5,000 drunks at St. Thomas Hospital
> in Akron. His spiritual example was a powerful influence, and he
> never charged a cent for his medical care. So Dr. Bob became *the*
> *prince of all twelfth-steppers*. Perhaps nobody will ever do such
> a job again (emphasis added).[3]

If you want to know what Dr. Bob did as he recovered from alcoholism and helped some 5,000 other alcoholics to achieve recovery, his reading defined a good part of the path. Of the path and
program that Dr. Bob and other early AAs followed, Frank Amos
reported: "He [the alcoholic] must have devotions every morning—a 'quiet time' of prayer and some reading from the Bible and
other religious literature. Unless this is faithfully followed, there

---

[2] (...continued)
way; 25% sobered up after some relapses, and among the remainder, those who stayed
on with A.A. showed improvement." Recently, A.A. historian, Charles Bishop, Jr.,
observed: "One survey question [by A.A. itself] revealed that out of 100 newcomers,
only 4 to 6 were able to maintain their newfound sobriety for a year. The vast majority
slipped. This was not the case in AA's early years." See Charlie Bishop, Jr., and Bill
Pittman, *To Be Continued. . . . The Alcoholics Anonymous World Bibliography 1935-*
1994 (WV: The Bishop of Books, 1994), p. xiii. In their title which shares their intensive
study of A.A.'s Big Book over many years, two A.A. old-timers said: "Half of all the
alcoholics who came to AA and seriously and sincerely tried to recover got sober
immediately and stayed that way. Another 25% sobered up a little more slowly. So in
the beginning, when the fellowship program and the program in the Big Book were the
same, it is estimated that 75% of the people who used the Twelve Step program and
really tried to recover from the disease of alcoholism actually did. We wonder what the
percentage is today. We doubt very seriously if it's 50 percent, let alone 75 percent."
See *A Program for You: A Guide to the Big Book's Design for Living* (MN: Hazelden,
1991), p. 15. And see Dick B., *New Light on Alcoholism: The A.A. Legacy from Sam*
Shoemaker (Corte Madera, CA: Good Book Publishing Company, 1994), p. 1—pointing
to the figures presented by A.A.'s current archivist and showing that one-third of A.A.
newcomers are out of the door within their first ninety days of A.A. participation.

[3] *The Co-Founders of Alcoholics Anonymous/Biographical Sketches. Their Last Major*
Talks (New York: Alcoholics Anonymous World Services, 1972, 1975), p. 27.

is grave danger of backsliding."[4] We therefore believe this study is vital to understanding Dr. Bob's successes.

About Reliance upon God

Clarence S. was one of those who came to Akron to be "fixed" by Dr. Bob. Clarence seemed initially to have had some doubts about "believing," but Dr. Bob confronted him squarely. He asked Clarence: "Do you believe in God, young fella?" When Clarence finally responded, "Yes, I do," Dr. Bob replied, "Now we are getting someplace. . . . Get out of bed and on your knees."[5] In other words, success in recovery in early A.A. was dependent upon belief in God. The Big Book itself later said, "We had to stop doubting the power of God" (p. 52). It added, "God either is, or He isn't. What was our choice to be" (p. 53)? When A.A.'s Big Book and later literature spoke of "came to believe," they were addressing the subject of finding God and experiencing His power.[6] Dr. Bob gave his explanation for it all: "Your Heavenly Father will never let you down!" (Big Book, p. 181).

And how can you and I confirm that? The keys can be found in Acts 17:11-12: ". . . [T]hey received the word with all readiness of mind, and searched the scriptures daily, whether those things were so. Therefore many of them believed. . . ."

THE END

---

[4] *DR. BOB*, p. 131.

[5] *DR. BOB*, pp. 142-44; Dick B., *That Amazing Grace: The Role of Clarence and Grace S. in Alcoholics Anonymous* (San Rafael, CA: Paradise Research Publications, 1996), pp. 25-26.

[6] See Big Book, pp. 45, 46, 56, 57; and see p. 59: "But there is One who has all power—that One is God. May you find Him now!"

Appendix 1

Dr. Bob's Biblical
and Christian Background

The Twelve Step and religious communities could much more easily grasp the significance of Dr. Bob's reading and studies, and of early A.A.'s biblical leanings and Christian fellowship, if they knew more about Dr. Bob's own background in that area. And this we have chosen to address in Appendix 1.

Dr. Bob's Comments about the Bible,
Church, & His Youth

In his last major address to Alcoholics Anonymous, at Detroit, Michigan, in December, 1948, Dr. Bob said of A.A.'s earliest and highly successful days:

> Now the interesting part of all this [the meeting of Bill W. and Dr. Bob] is not the sordid details, but the situation we two fellows were in. We had both been associated with the Oxford Group, Bill in New York, for five months, and I in Akron, for two and a half years. Bill had acquired their idea of service. I had not, but I had done an immense amount of reading they had recommended. *I had refreshed my memory of the Good Book* [the Bible], *and I had had excellent training in that as a youngster*. They said that I should affiliate myself with some church, and we did that. They said that I should cultivate the habit of prayer, and I did that—at least, to a considerable extent for me (emphasis added).[7]

> At that point ["in early A.A. days"], our stories didn't amount to anything to speak of. When we [Bill Wilson and Dr. Bob] started in on Bill D. [A.A. No. 3], we had no Twelve Steps, either; we had no Traditions. But *we were convinced that the answer to our problems was in the Good Book* [the Bible]. To some of us older ones, the parts we found absolutely essential were the Sermon

---

[7] *The Co-Founders of Alcoholics Anonymous: Biographical Sketches, Their Last Major Talks* (New York: Alcoholics Anonymous World Services, Inc., 1972, 1975), pp. 11-12.

on the Mount, the thirteenth chapter of First Corinthians, and the Book of James (emphasis added).[8]

It wasn't until 1938 that the teachings and efforts and studies that had been going on were crystallized in the form of the Twelve Steps. I didn't write the Twelve Steps. I had nothing to do with the writing of them. But I think I probably had something to do with them indirectly. After my June 10th episode [the date of Dr. Bob's last drink], Bill came to live at our house and stayed for about three months. There was hardly a night that we didn't sit up until two or three o'clock, talking. It would be hard for me to conceive that, during these nightly discussions around our kitchen table, nothing was said that influenced the writing of the Twelve Steps. *We already had the basic ideas, though not in terse and tangible form. We got them, as I said, as a result of our study of the Good Book* (emphasis added).[9]

In his personal story, carried in each edition of the Big Book, Dr. Bob said:

From childhood through high school I was more or less forced to go to *church*, *Sunday School* and *evening service*, Monday night *Christian Endeavor* and sometimes to *Wednesday evening prayer meeting* (Big Book, 3rd ed., p. 172, emphasis added).

[Of his Oxford Group affiliation prior to the time he got sober] I sensed they had something I did not have, from which I might readily profit. I learned that it was something of a spiritual nature, which did not appeal to me very much, but I thought it could do no harm. I gave the matter much time and study for the next two and a half years, but still got tight every night nevertheless. I read everything I could find, and talked to everyone who I thought knew anything about it (Big Book, 3rd ed., p. 178).

The Story of Christian Endeavor

Dr. Bob said that he had attended Christian Endeavor, and this prompted the author to find out just what Christian Endeavor did and what reading was involved in that. And a good starting place was with the "Official Edition" of *Christian Endeavor in All Lands*. This title was written by the Reverend Francis E. Clark, D.D., LL.D., the Founder of the Christian Endeavor Movement. Of the Christian roots of the Endeavor movement, Clark said:

The roots of the Christian Endeavor tree, wherever it grows, are Confession of Christ, Service for Christ, Fellowship with Christ's people, and Loyalty to Christ's Church. The farther I travel, the more I see of societies in every land,

---

[8] *The Co-Founders*, supra, p. 13.

[9] *The Co-Founders*, supra, p. 14.

the more I am convinced that these four principles are the essential and the only essential principles of the Christian Endeavor Society. Let me repeat them:—I. Confession of Christ. II. Service for Christ. III. Fellowship with Christ's people. IV. Loyalty to Christ's Church (*Christian Endeavor in All Lands*, p. 93).

Then, as to the first principle—Confession of Christ—Clark wrote:

> I. *Confession of Christ* is absolutely necessary in the Christian Endeavor Society. . . . Every week comes the prayer meeting, in which every member who fulfills his vow must take some part. . . . This participation is simply the confession of Christ. The true Christian Endeavorer does not take part to exhibit his rhetoric, or to gain practice in public speaking, or to show what a logical prayer he can offer to God; but he does take part to show that he is a Christian, to confess his love for the Lord. . . . The covenant pledge is simply a tried and proved devise to secure frequent confession of Christ. . . . It also secures familiarity with the Word of God by promoting Bible-reading and study in pre-paration for every meeting (*Christian Endeavor, supra*, pp. 94, 96).

Clark also quoted the Reverend F. B. Meyer, who not only had a substantial later influence on the Oxford Group and on early A.A. ideas, but was also president of the British Christian Endeavor Union. Clark quoted F. B. Meyer as follows:

> Christian Endeavor stands for five great principles: (1) Personal devotion to the divine Lord and Saviour, Jesus Christ. . . . (2) The covenant obligation embodied in our pledge. . . . (3) Constant religious training for all kinds of service. . . . (4) Strenuous loyalty to the local church and denomination with which each society is connected. (5) Interdenominational spiritual fellowship (*Christian Endeavor, supra*, pp. 101-02).

Clark said the following represented a simple form of the much-mentioned "covenant.":

> Trusting in the Lord Jesus for strength, I promise him that I will strive to do whatever He would like to have me do; that I will pray and read the Bible every day; and that, just so far as I know how, I will endeavor to lead a Christian life. I will be present at every meeting of the society, unless prevented by some reason which I can conscientiously give to my Saviour, and will take part in the meeting, either by prayer, testimony, or a Bible verse. As an active member of t his society I promise to be faithful to my own church, and to do all I can to uphold its works and membership (*Christian Endeavor, supra*, p. 252).

According to the Reverend Clark, "Every Endeavor meeting has its topic, with many Scripture references and abundant helps" (*Christian Endeavor, supra*, p. 261). He then mentioned and recommended a Christian Endeavor text-book written by Amos R. Wells, Editorial Secretary of the United Society of Christian Endeavor. The book which Wells wrote was titled, *Expert Endeavor: A Text-book of Christian Endeavor Methods and*

Principles. And the following are some of the things Wells wrote about "the prayer meeting":

> **What are the results we may gain from the prayer meeting?** They are five: original thought on religious subjects: open committal to the cause of Christ; the helpful expression of Christian thought and experience; the cultivation of the spirit of worship through public prayer and through singing; the guidance of others along these lines of service and life (p. 9).

> **How can we get original thought on the prayer-meeting topics?** Only by study of the Bible, followed by meditation and observation. First, the Endeavorer should read the Bible passage; then he should read some good commentary upon it; then he should take the subject with him into his daily life for five or six days, thinking about it in his odd minutes and watching for experiences in his own life or the lives of others, or observing nature and looking for illustrations on the subject from all these sources (pp. 9-10).

> **Are we to read Bible verses and other quotations?** Yes, all we please, if we will make them the original expression of our own lives by thinking about them, and adding to them something, if only a sentence, to show that we have made them our own. Always give the writer's name, or the part of the Bible from which you quote. Commit the quotation to memory and do not read it (p. 11).

A.A.'s own *DR. BOB and the Good Oldtimers* states many things about the Bible study, prayer and meditation practices of Dr. Bob that seem to ring very clearly back to what has been set forth above about his "excellent training" in the Bible as a youngster and his familiarity with the Good Book. In fact, at a recent talk, the author met a woman who had been an active member of Christian Endeavor. She pointed out that she had actually memorized and presented the entire Book of Romans at a Christian Endeavor meeting. She said everyone had a job, that there was tremendous support for the local church, and that there were frequent gatherings of groups of churches in her area.

Some of the things that Christian Endeavor did, and which seem harbingers of what Dr. Bob himself did are these: (1) Daily Bible study; (2) Daily prayer; (3) Daily meditation on some subject raised in the Bible or Christian commentary; (4) Frequent quoting from the Bible; (5) Confession of Jesus Christ as Lord and Saviour; (6) Living Christian principles; (7) Guidance of others; (8) Gathering together for Bible study, prayer, and Christian fellowship; (9) Witnessing; (10) Loyalty to, and affiliation with, a Christian church. And, though Dr. Bob himself spoke as though he had seldom, after his youth, darkened the door of a church, the facts are quite to the contrary as he moved into serious alcoholism and then sobriety and the foundation of the A.A. Fellowship.

The Story of Dr. Bob's Church Affiliations

It is appropriate to say, at the beginning, that there are perhaps three different views of Dr. Bob's church activities.

First, that, as a youth, he was intensely involved with church activities at St. Johnsbury, Vermont. And this was because of his parents' immense involvement. Second, that Dr. Bob had apparently been subjected to overload in that period of his life, as far as the church-going was concerned. To what degree Dr. Bob had a distaste for such activities at the end of his younger years is hard to say. One the one hand, he said he resolved never again to darken the door of a church. On the other, he said he had had excellent training in the Bible as a young person. Also, when he was married and had a family, he very definitely was involved in taking his kids to Sunday school and also in church membership himself. Third, Dr. Bob's view, at the later point in his life, is possibly best summarized by the statement of his son "Smitty" to the author: Dr. Bob was more interested in the "message" than the "messenger." For he certainly studied the Bible, prayed for himself and others, and meditated on the Bible and Christian literature and in expectant waiting for the guidance of God in his daily life.

North Congregational Church in St. Johnsbury, Vermont

Dr. Bob's son Smitty told the author, and A.A.'s own history records, that Dr. Bob's parents were "pillars" of the North Congregational Church in St. Johnsbury, Vermont. Dr. Bob himself spoke of being more or less forced, as a youth, to go to church. When asked recently by the author, his daughter Sue Smith Windows, told the author that she could not help but believe that Dr. Bob was much involved in the North Congregational Church in Vermont because of his mother's insistent influence. Furthermore, while expressing a later distaste for church, Dr. Bob nonetheless, returned later to *several* Protestant Christian churches; talked of his excellent training, quite clearly in the North Congregational Church and Christian Endeavor; and followed through on the intense Bible study, prayer, and meditation he had learned as a youth. This later commitment was, of course, very much enhanced by the suggestions and practices of the Oxford Group. And they continued throughout his sobriety.

St. Luke's Protestant Episcopal Church?

In a recent telephone conversation with the author, Dr. Bob's son said he believed his dad had belonged to St. Luke's Church before the affiliations about to be discussed. However, he suggested a check with his sister Sue Smith Windows. Sue said she had never heard of that church; so that particular affiliation is in need of further investigation, if it existed at all.

Church of Our Saviour Protestant Episcopal Church

Dr. Bob's daughter Sue was very clear, in her recent phone conversation with the author, that she and her brother ("Smitty") were regular attenders at the Church of Our Saviour in the Akron, Ohio, area. She told the author the church was located at the corner of Oakdale and Crosby Streets. While she could not verify that her dad belonged to the church, she believed he probably did because "We got to the Church of Our Saviour Sunday School somehow." Perhaps St. Luke's and Church of Our Saviour merge into one Episcopal Church membership by Dr. Bob before he got sober; but this will have to await further research, possibly by the author during a visit to Akron.

One thing seems almost certain, and that is that Dr. Bob belonged to one or the other of the two churches before he got sober and possibly after January, 1933. He said that he had joined a church, during his drinking period, at the suggestion of the Oxford Group people with whom he and Anne were then meeting regularly. His children, now eighty years old, seem to remember little of this church period except that they were taken to Sunday School by Dr. Bob.

Westminster United Presbyterian Church in Akron

The author personally verified that Dr. Bob and his wife Anne became charter members of the Westminster United Presbyterian Church in Akron, Ohio, by "letter of transfer." They joined the church on June 3, 1936, slightly less than a year after Dr. Bob got sober. They remained members of that church until April 3, 1942. The interesting thing about this membership period is the exchange that the pastor had with Sam Shoemaker by letter to Sam in New York, reporting on how well things were going in Akron "since Wilson was here." Obviously, therefore, both Shoemaker and the pastor of the Presbyterian Church were conversant with Bob's problems and with Bill's successful meeting with Bob in the summer of 1935.

St. Paul's Protestant Episcopal Church in Akron

Contrary to what some histories say, there was no membership in this church by Dr. Bob's wife. The rector, Dr. Richard McCandless, confirmed this in the author's presence during the author's visit to St. Paul's church in Akron. However, the rector also confirmed that Dr. Bob did become a communicant at St. Paul's Protestant Episcopal Church in Akron before he died.

This church has great significance in A.A. history because its rector was Dr. Walter Tunks. Tunks was Harvey Firestone, Sr.,'s pastor. He was a substantial participant in the events that brought Oxford Group Founder Dr. Frank Buchman to Akron in the famous events of January, 1933. Tunks performed several liturgical services involving Dr. Bob's family; and the link of A.A. to St. Paul's seemed to last, one way or the other, from the earliest days in 1933 to the date of Dr. Bob's death.[10]

The Christian Outfall

Early A.A. Surrenders to Christ

While the *precise* details of the Christian "surrenders" that occurred in early A.A. are somewhat murky, there has been general agreement that several things were involved:

First, the new AA accepted Jesus Christ as his Lord and Savior. Oldtimer Larry B. specifically told the author on the telephone several years ago that when he (Larry) went

---

[10] See discussion in Dick B., *The Akron Genesis*, p. 30.

upstairs to surrender, he "got born again." Clarence Snyder told his wife Grace and a number of his sponsees that surrenders involved the "Sinner's Prayer" and a new birth.[11] Bill Van H. introduced Clarence Snyder to, and popularized 2 Corinthians 5:17:

> Therefore if any man *be* in Christ, *he is* a new creature: old things are passed away; behold, all things are become new.[12]

The specifics will have to be left at that unless further evidence or records surface.

Dr. Bob Was Himself a Christian

A number of uninformed writers have claimed that Dr. Bob was not a Christian, but a reading of their comments makes clear that they have neither seen nor reviewed the evidence in this or the author's other titles.

Dr. Bob's life in St. Johnsbury is proof enough by itself that Dr. Bob was a Christian. His involvement in Christian Endeavor puts an exclamation point to the proof. His involvement in at least three other Christian churches—two Episcopalian Churches and one Presbyterian Church—certainly indicates his confession at the church level. His daughter Sue stated to the author, at his first interview with her, that her father was a Christian. Dr. Bob regularly referred to the early A.A. meetings as Christian Fellowship meetings. There the Bible was read, the Lord's Prayer was recited, and surrenders to Christ occurred with Dr. Bob leading them and the newcomer acceding. Dr. Bob was not only a Christian, but a strong "ambassador for Christ."[13]

While the exact form has not yet been located by the author, it seems a strong probability that Dr. Bob and his wife Anne regularly recited the Apostle's Creed at every service at the Westminster United Presbyterian Church in Akron during Bob's charter membership there. That creed, though having various forms, has been authoritatively been set forth as follows:

> I believe in God the Father Almighty, Maker of heaven and earth; And in Jesus Christ, His only Son, our Lord; who was conceived by the Holy Ghost, born of the Virgin Mary; suffered under Pontius Pilate, was crucified, dead, and buried;

---

[11] See Dick B., *That Amazing Grace: The Role of Clarence and Grace Snyder in Alcoholics Anonymous* (San Rafael, CA: Paradise Research Publications, 1996), pp. 52, 68, 83, 92-93; Clarence Snyder, *Going Through The Steps*, 2d ed. (Altamonte Springs, FL: Stephen F. Foreman, 1985), pp. 2-3; Mitch K., one of Clarence's sponsees, so informed the author at an interview in West Virginia; Clancy U. is Hawaii, who was a sponsee of both Dr. Bob and Clarence, spoke of the same thing; so did oldtimer Ed Andy.

[12] See Dick B., *That Amazing Grace*, *supra*, pp. 33-34.

[13] 2 Corinthians 5:20-21: "Now then we are ambassadors for Christ, as though God did beseech *you* by us: we pray *you* in Christ's stead, be ye reconciled to God. For he hath made him *to be* sin for us, who knew no sin; that we might be made the righteousness of God in him."

He descended into Hades; the third day he rose from the dead. He ascended into heaven, and sitteth on the right hand of God the Father Almighty; from thence he shall come to judge the quick and the dead. And I believe in the Holy Ghost; the holy Catholic Church; the communion of saints; the forgiveness of sins; the resurrection of the body; and the life everlasting.[14]

Though there may denominational disagreements concerning the wording and meaning of the foregoing language, the recital of it certainly brings one within the specifications of Mark 16:15-16, Acts 2:16-36, 3:12-26, 4:8-14, 10:34-48, 13:26-49, 17:2-4, 11-12, 19:1-7, Romans 10:9-10. And the confession with the mouth and belief in the heart establishes his or her new birth and salvation.

The Surrenders Were Based on the Practices in James

Early AAs considered the Book of James their favorite. James 5:13-16 states:

Is any among you afflicted? let him pray. Is any merry? let him sing psalms. Is any sick among you? let him call for the elders of the church; and let them pray over him, anointing him with oil in the name of the Lord: And the prayer of faith shall save the sick, and the Lord shall raise him up; and if he have committed sins, they shall be forgiven him. Confess *your* faults one to another, and pray for one another, that ye may be healed. The effectual fervent prayer of a righteous man availeth much.

According to Mitch K., one of Clarence S.'s sponsees, this process was followed when a man made surrender. He was brought to Christ in this fashion. Others have disputed that there was anointing with oil in the early surrenders. Several versions can be found in *DR. BOB and the Good Oldtimers* (pp. 131, 137-44). But T. Henry Williams, who was not an alcoholic, and was present at most of the early surrenders, said this:

After the meeting, we might take the new man upstairs, and a group of men would ask him to surrender his life to God and start in to really live up to the four absolutes and also to go out and help the other men who needed it. This was in the form of a prayer group. Several of the boys would pray together, and the new man would make his own prayer, asking God to take alcohol out of his life, and when he was through, he would say, "Thank you, God, for taking it out of my life." During the prayer, he usually made a declaration of his willingness to turn his life over to God."[15]

---

[14] Philip Schaff, *History of the Christian Church, Volume II, Ante-Nicene Christianity, A.D. 100-325* (Grand Rapids, MI: Wm B. Eerdmans Publishing Company, 1910), p. 537.

[15] *DR. BOB*, p. 139.

Because of the immense amount of editorial resistance to Jesus Christ in official A.A. accounts, it is very difficult to do more than quote the various oldtimers who affirmed that one became a Christian when he surrendered "upstairs" in Akron with the group of men who prayed over him, for him, and with him.

The End Result Was a Christian Fellowship

The Oxford Group, of which early A.A. was an integral part in Akron and in New York, was definitely known as *A First Century Christian Fellowship*.[16] Dr. Bob called early A.A. "A Christian Fellowship."[17] And it was!

---

[16] Samuel M. Shoemaker, *Twice-Born Ministers* (New York: Fleming H. Revell, 1929), pp. 23, 46, 90, 95, 101, 122, 147, 148; *Calvary Church Yesterday and Today* (New York: Fleming H. Revell Company, 1936), pp. 270-72; *A First-Century Christian Fellowship: A Defense of So-Called Buchmanism by One of Its Leaders* (Reprinted from *The Churchman*, 1928).

[17] *DR. BOB*, p. 118. Dr. Bob's daughter, Sue Smith Windows, informed the author in an interview that Dr. Bob called every A.A. meeting a "Christian Fellowship." Bob E. wrote Lois Wilson a note to the same effect.

Appendix 2

Inventory of Books on Hand at
Calvary House, September 12, 1933 *

(List found at the Archives of the Episcopal Church U.S.A., Austin, Texas)

An Apostle to Youth (old style) [John McCook Roots]
An Apostle to Youth [John McCook Roots]
Guidance of God [Eleanor Forde]
Principles of the Group [Sherwood S. Day]
Sharing [Julian P. Thornton-Duesbury]
How to Find Reality [Donald W. Carruthers]
Quiet Time [Howard Rose]
Three Levels of Life [Samuel Shoemaker]
Letter #7 [1930]
A Med. Oxford Group *
One Boy's Influence [Samuel Shoemaker]
The Church and the Oxford Groups *
Stories of Our Oxford Group H. P. *
Jesus Christ and Mental Health *
Groups Came to Louisville *
What If I Had But One Sermon to Preach [Samuel Shoemaker]
Meaning of Conversion *
It Turned out to Be a Revival *
For Doubters Only *
Group Leadership *
A First Century Christian Fellowship *
Oxford Group in Aberdeen *
Seek Ye First *
Atlantic Monthly, Dec., 1928 *
The Group Stirs Religious Life in Asheville *
The Student, the Fish and Agassiz *
The First Century Ch. Fellowship Today *
For Sinners Only (American) [A. J. Russell]
For Sinners Only (English) [A. J. Russell]
He That Cometh [Geoffrey Francis Hallen]

121

The Conversion of the Church [Samuel Shoemaker]
Life Changers [Harold Begbie]
Children of the Second Birth [Samuel Shoemaker]
Twice Born Ministers [Samuel Shoemaker]
Soul Surgery [H. A. Walter]
Realizing Religion [Samuel Shoemaker]
A Young Man's View of the Ministry [Samuel Shoemaker]
Religion That Works [Samuel Shoemaker]
If I Be Lifted Up [Samuel Shoemaker]
Confident Faith [Samuel Shoemaker]
Seeking and Finding [Ebenezer Macmillan]
For Sinners Only (German)
Unter Gottes Fuhrun *
God in the Slums *
God in the Shadows *
Moffatt N. T.
New Lives for Old [Amelia S. Reynolds]
Creative Prayer [E. Herman]
Time, June 8, 1931
Londay Daily Express, April 16, 1932
Akron Times Press, January 21, 1933
Misc. Amer. newspapers--Dec. 1932-Feb. 1933
Church of Eng. newspapers misc. 1932
Church of Eng. newspapers, old files of M. Reynolds
Church of Eng. newspapers, June 3, 1932
Church of Eng. newspapers, July 8, 1932
Church of Eng. newspapers, July 15, 1932
Sunday Referee, July 12, 1931
Misc. English papers, 1932
Detroit Free Press, May 28, 1932
Los Angeles Times, Feb. 6-8, 1933
Development of the Group in Average Parish
"Things Old and New" (*Christian Observer*)
"Things in Common" (*Christian Observer*)
"Moral Content" (*Christian Observer*)
Sunday Chronicle, Mar. 13, 1932
The Work of Frank Buchman--one large box of papers, Detroit, KC, Louisville
Article by Russell (C. O.), Oct. 21, 1931
First Cent. Ch. Fell. by S. M. S., Jr.
Happy Am I
Group System in the Catholic Church
Cleve Hicks' Bible Study Lessons

* Copies of these books have not yet been located.

Index

A

A.A. Archives 3, 8, 19, 22

AA The Way It Began (Pittman, Bill) 3, 12, 32, 33, 36, 37, 40, 42, 46, 54, 56, 59, 67

Abundant Living (Jones, E. Stanley) 34, 69, 89

Akron Genesis of Alcoholics Anonymous, The (B., Dick) 2, 4, 32, 58, 87

Alcoholic squad (of the Oxford Group) 5, 10, 18

Allen, Geoffrey (*He That Cometh*) 46

Allen, James 13, 18, 23, 56, 57, 88

  As a Man Thinketh 23, 56, 60

  Heavenly Life 57, 88

Almighty God 50

Almond, Harry J. (*Foundations for Faith*) 91

Along the Indian Road (Jones, E. Stanley) 68, 69

Alter Your Life (Fox, Emmet) 68

Amos, Frank B. 12, 15, 43, 108, 113

Apostle James, The 8

Apostle Paul, The 8, 44, 101

Apostle's Creed 117

Art of Living, The (Peale, Norman Vincent) 76, 88

Art of Selfishness, The (Seabury, David) 76

As a Man Thinketh (Allen, James) 23, 56, 60

As I See Religion (Fosdick, Harry Emerson) 65

Atonement 18, 49, 67

Authors of Special Interest (to Dr. Bob) 35, 37, 56

B

B., Dick

  Akron Genesis of Alcoholics Anonymous, The 2, 4, 32, 58, 87

  Books Early AAs Read for Spiritual Growth, The 2, 79, 87

  New Light on Alcoholism: The A. A. Legacy from Sam Shoemaker 2, 24, 49, 53, 55, 79, 80, 87, 99, 108

  Oxford Group & Alcoholics Anonymous, The 2, 10, 30, 49, 79, 87, 99

B., Mel (A.A. member--author, *New Wine*) 9, 17, 30, 37, 42, 63, 66, 72

Barbanelle, Maurice (*Parish the Healer*) 77

Barton, George A. (*Jesus of Nazareth*) 29

Basic ideas (A.A.) 1, 9, 16, 95, 100, 107, 112

Basic Teachings of Confucius, The (Dawson, Miles) 76

H

I

J

Y

Dick B.'s Historical Titles on Early A.A.'s Spiritual Roots and Successes

Dr. Bob and His Library: A Major A.A. Spiritual Source (Third Edition)
Foreword by Ernest Kurtz, Ph.D., Author, *Not-God: A History of Alcoholics Anonymous.*

A study of the immense spiritual reading of the Bible, Christian literature, and Oxford Group books done and recommended by A.A. co-founder, Dr. Robert H. Smith. Paradise Research Publications, Inc.; 156 pp.; 6 x 9; perfect bound; $15.95; 1998; ISBN 1-885803-25-7.

Anne Smith's Journal, 1933-1939: A.A.'s Principles of Success (Third Edition)
Foreword by Robert R. Smith, son of Dr. Bob & Anne Smith; co-author, *Children of the Healer.*

Dr. Bob's wife, Anne, kept a journal in the 1930's from which she shared with early AAs and their families ideas from the Bible and the Oxford Group. Her ideas substantially influenced A.A.'s program. Paradise Research Publications, Inc.; 180 pp.; 6 x 9; perfect bound; 1998; $16.95; ISBN 1-885803-24-9.

The Oxford Group & Alcoholics Anonymous (Second Edition)
Foreword by Rev. T. Willard Hunter; author, columnist, Oxford Group activist.

A comprehensive history of the origins, principles, practices, and contributions to A.A. of "A First Century Christian Fellowship" (also known as the Oxford Group) of which A.A. was an integral part in the developmental period between 1931 and 1939. Paradise Research Publications, Inc.; 432 pp.; 6 x 9; perfect bound; 1998; $17.95; ISBN 1-885803-19-2.(Previous title: *Design for Living*).

The Akron Genesis of Alcoholics Anonymous (Newton Edition)
Foreword by former U.S. Congressman John F. Seiberling of Akron, Ohio.

The story of A.A.'s birth at Dr. Bob's Home in Akron on June 10, 1935. Tells what early AAs did in their meetings, homes, and hospital visits; what they read; how their ideas developed from the Bible, Oxford Group, and Christian literature. Depicts roles of A.A. founders and their wives; Henrietta Seiberling; and T. Henry Williams. Paradise Research Pub.; 400 pp., 6 x 9; perfect bound; 1998; $17.95; ISBN 1-885803-17-6.

The Books Early AAs Read for Spiritual Growth (Fwd. by John Seiberling; 7th Ed.)
The most exhaustive bibliography (with brief summaries) of all the books known to have been read and recommended for spiritual growth by early AAs in Akron and on the East Coast. Paradise Research Publications, Inc.; 126 pp.; 6 x 9; perfect bound; 1998; $15.95; ISBN 1-885803-26-5.

New Light on Alcoholism: The A.A. Legacy from Sam Shoemaker
Forewords by Nickie Shoemaker Haggart, daughter of Rev. Sam Shoemaker; and Mrs. W. Irving Harris.

A comprehensive history and analysis of the all-but-forgotten specific contributions to A.A. spiritual principles and practices by New York's famous Episcopal preacher, the Rev. Dr. Samuel M. Shoemaker, Jr.—dubbed by Bill W. a "co-founder" of A.A. and credited by Bill as the well-spring of A.A.'s spiritual recovery ideas. Good Book Publishing Company; 416 pp.; 6 x 9; perfect bound; 1994; $19.95; ISBN 1-881212-06-8.

The Good Book and The Big Book: A.A.'s Roots in the Bible (Bridge Builders Ed.)
Foreword by Robert R. Smith, son of Dr. Bob & Anne Smith; co-author, *Children of the Healer.*

The author shows conclusively that A.A.'s program of recovery came primarily from the Bible. This is a history of A.A.'s biblical roots as they can be seen in A.A.'s Big Book, Twelve Steps, and Fellowship. Paradise Research Publications, Inc.; 264 pp.; 6 x 9; perfect bound; 1997; $17.95; ISBN 1-885803-16-8.

That Amazing Grace: The Role of Clarence and Grace S. in Alcoholics Anonymous
Foreword by Harold E. Hughes, former U.S. Senator from, and Governor of, Iowa.

Precise details of early A.A.'s spiritual practices—from the recollections of Grace S., widow of A.A. pioneer, Clarence S. Paradise Research Pub; 160 pp.; 6 x 9; perfect bound; 1996; $16.95; ISBN 1-885803-06-0.

Good Morning!: Quiet Time, Morning Watch, Meditation, and Early A.A.
A practical guide to Quiet Time—considered a "must" in early A.A. Discusses biblical roots, history, helpful books, and how to. Paradise Research Pub; 154 pp.; 6 x 9; perf. bound; 1998; $15.50; ISBN: 1-885803-09-5.

Turning Point: A History of Early A.A.'s Spiritual Roots and Successes
Foreword by Paul Wood, Ph.D., President, National Council on Alcoholism and Drug Dependence.

Turning Point is a comprehensive history of early A.A.'s spiritual roots and successes. It is the culmination of six years of research, traveling, and interviews. Dick B.'s latest title shows specifically what the Twelve Step pioneers borrowed from: (1) The Bible; (2) The Rev. Sam Shoemaker's teachings; (3) The Oxford Group; (4) Anne Smith's Journal; and (5) meditation periodicals and books, such as *The Upper Room*. Paradise Research Publications, Inc.; 776 pp.; 6 x 9; perfect bound; 1997; $29.95; ISBN: 1-885803-07-9.

Inquiries, orders, and requests for
catalogs and discount schedules
should be addressed to:

Dick B.
c/o Good Book Publishing Company
Box 837
Kihei, Maui, Hawaii 96753-0837
1-808-874-4876 (phone & fax)
email: dickb@dickb.com
Internet Web Site: "http://www.dickb.com"

About the Author

Dick B. writes books on the spiritual roots of Alcoholics Anonymous. They show how the basic and highly successful biblical ideas used by early AAs can be valuable tools for success in today's A.A. His research can also help the religious and recovery communities work more effectively with alcoholics, addicts, and others involved in Twelve Step programs.

The author is an active, recovered member of A.A.; a retired attorney; and a Bible student. He has sponsored more than seventy men in their recovery from alcoholism. Consistent with A.A.'s traditions of anonymity, he uses the pseudonym "Dick B."

He has had thirteen titles published: *Dr. Bob's Library*; *Anne Smith's Journal, 1933-1939*; *Design for Living: The Oxford Group's Contribution to Early A.A.*; *The Akron Genesis of Alcoholics Anonymous*; *The Books Early AAs Read for Spiritual Growth*; *New Light on Alcoholism: The A.A. Legacy from Sam Shoemaker*; *Courage to Change* (with Bill Pittman); *The Good Book and The Big Book: A.A.'s Roots in the Bible*; *That Amazing Grace: The Role of Clarence and Grace S. in Alcoholics Anonymous*; *Good Morning!: Quiet Time, Morning Watch, Meditation, and Early A.A.*; *Turning Point: A History of Early A.A.'s Spiritual Roots and Successes, Hope!: The Story of Geraldine D., Alina Lodge & Recovery*, and *Utilizing Early A.A.'s Spiritual Roots for Recovery Today*. The books have been the subject of newspaper articles, and have been reviewed in *Library Journal, Bookstore Journal, For a Change, The Living Church, Faith at Work, Sober Times, Episcopal Life, Recovery News, Ohioana Quarterly, The PHOENIX, MRA Newsletter*, and the *Saint Louis University Theology Digest*.

Dick is the father of two married sons (Ken and Don) and a grandfather. As a young man, he did a stint as a newspaper reporter. He attended the University of California, Berkeley, where he received his A.A. degree, majored in economics, and was elected to Phi Beta Kappa in his Junior year. In the United States Army, he was an Information-Education Specialist. He received his A.B. and J.D. degrees from Stanford University, and was Case Editor of the Stanford Law Review. Dick became interested in Bible study in his childhood Sunday School and was much inspired by his mother's almost daily study of Scripture. He joined, and was president of, a Community Church affiliated with the United Church of Christ. By 1972, he was studying the origins of the Bible and began traveling abroad in pursuit of that subject. In 1979, he became much involved in a Biblical research, teaching, and fellowship ministry. In his community life, he was president of a merchants' council, Chamber of Commerce, church retirement center, and homeowners' association. He served on a public district board and was active in a service club.

In 1986, he was felled by alcoholism, gave up his law practice, and began recovery as a member of the Fellowship of Alcoholics Anonymous. In 1990, his interest in A.A.'s Biblical/Christian roots was sparked by his attendance at A.A.'s International Convention in Seattle. He has traveled widely; researched at archives, and at public and seminary libraries; interviewed scholars, historians, clergy, A.A. "old-timers" and survivors; and participated in programs on A.A.'s roots.

The author is the owner of Good Book Publishing Company and has several works in progress. Much of his research and writing is done in collaboration with his older son, Ken, who holds B.A., B.Th., and M.A. degrees. Ken has been a lecturer in New Testament Greek at a Bible college and a lecturer in Fundamentals of Oral Communication at San Francisco State University. Ken is a computer specialist.

Dick is a member of the American Historical Association, Maui Writers Guild, and The Authors' Guild. He is available for conferences, panels, seminars, and interviews.

How to Order Dick B.'s Historical Titles on Early A.A.

Order Form

Qty.

Send:

__ *Turning Point* (a comprehensive history)	@ $29.95 ea.	$_____
__ *New Light on Alcoholism* (Sam Shoemaker)	@ $19.95 ea.	$_____
__ *The Oxford Group & Alcoholics Anonymous*	@ $17.95 ea.	$_____
__ *The Good Book and The Big Book* (Bible roots)	@ $17.95 ea.	$_____
__ *The Akron Genesis of Alcoholics Anonymous*	@ $17.95 ea.	$_____
__ *That Amazing Grace* (Clarence and Grace S.)	@ $16.95 ea.	$_____
__ *Good Morning!* (Quiet Time, etc.)	@ $16.95 ea.	$_____
__ *Anne Smith's Journal, 1933-1939*	@ $16.95 ea.	$_____
__ *Books Early AAs Read for Spiritual Growth*	@ $15.95 ea.	$_____
__ *Dr. Bob and His Library*	@ $15.95 ea.	$_____

Shipping and Handling (S & H) **   Subtotal $_____

Add 10% of retail price (minimum US$3.75). ** U.S. only.
For "The Set," add US$18.67. ** U.S. only   **S & H** $_____
Please call, fax, or email for shipments outside the U.S.

Total Enclosed $_____

Name: _____ (as it appears on your credit card)

Address: _____

City: _____ State: _____ Zip: _____

Credit Card #: _____ (MC VISA AMEX) **Exp.** _____

Tel. #: _____ Signature _____

Email address: _____

Special Value for You!

If purchased separately, the author's ten titles sell for US$186.70, plus Shipping and Handling. Using this Order Form, you may purchase sets of all ten titles for **only $149.95 per set, plus US$18.67** Shipping and Handling. Please contact us for Shipping and Handling charges for orders being shipped outside of the United States.

Send Order Form (or copy), with check or money order, to: Dick B., P.O. Box 837, Kihei, HI 96753-0837. Please make check or money order payable to **"Dick B."** in U.S. dollars drawn on a U.S. bank. For questions, please phone or fax: 1-808-874-4876. Our email: dickb@dickb.com. **Dick B.'s Web Site:** "http://www.dickb.com".